A TREATISE ON AFFLICTIONS

Thomas Case

Edited by Dr. Gerald Mick

DIGITAL 𝔓uritan PRESS

Digital Puritan Press
1021 Watertown Drive
Westfield, Indiana, 46074
USA

www.digitalpuritan.net

ISBN 978-1466499614

Follow *The Digital Puritan* on Facebook or Twitter. Please address e-mail correspondence to info@digitalpuritan.net.

This title is also available as an e-book in many popular formats. See www.digitalpuritan.net for more information.

Cover Art: Jan Pietruszka.

Library of Congress Cataloging-in-Publication Data

Case, Thomas, 1598-1682.
    A treatise on afflictions / by Thomas Case ; edited by Gerald Mick.
        p. cm.
    Rev. ed. of: Correction, instruction: or, the rod and the word.
    Includes index.
    ISBN 978-1466499614
    1. Suffering—Sermons. I. Mick, Gerald. II. Title.
BV4909 .C373 2011
248.32—dc23

                                2011944863
                                CIP

vulgo vetus veritas

CONTENTS

BIOGRAPHICAL PREFACE

THOMAS CASE was born in the county of Kent, in England. He was the son of Mr. George Case, Minister of Boxley in that county. His father, who was eminently distinguished both by his parts and his piety, was peculiarly attentive to him, and gave him a well-directed and religious education in early life, which is commonly the best time for instruction. "Train up a child in the way he should go; and when he is old he will not depart from it" (Proverbs 22:6). The importance of early instruction is written upon the whole system of nature, and repeated in every page of the history of providence. You may bend a young twig and make it receive almost any form; but that which has attained to maturity, and taken its ply, you will never bring into another shape than that which it naturally bears. Children may undoubtedly receive much benefit by the use of means, in a very early period of life. And when parents use the means, they ought carefully to remember the beautiful connection between the duty and the promise, "Train up a child in the way he should go; and when he is old he will not depart from it." We ought to believe the certainty of the promise, as well as the obligation of the duty, so taking a full view of the connection.

The beautiful connection here was very clearly seen in the pious subject of these pages. Under the seasonable and wholesome instruction of a religious and careful father, accompanied with the divine blessing, the amiable and tractable son, drinking in spiritual and good instructions with much earnestness and delight, gave very signal proofs of his eminently pious disposition, and of his great ingenuity, even in his childhood, upon the first dawn of reason, which continued with him until old age.

We are informed that he was a very young convert, and that his conversion began with prayer in very early life, "God working in him both to will and to do of his good pleasure" (Philippians 2:13), when he was only six years of age. The solemn transaction with the Lord God of his salvation appears to have been very deeply engraved upon his young mind; for he himself related it to Dr. Jacomb, who preached his funeral sermon.

And at that age, through the influence of divine grace, he was inclined to pray by himself every morning and evening, showing forth with a grateful heart the loving-kindness of God in promising salvation in the morning, and his faithfulness in accomplishing it every night, which are inexhaustible subjects for morning and evening prayers and praises. And he prayed not by the help of any book or form, either read or remembered, but by the gracious assistance of the Holy Spirit. He readily performed the duty, not upon any precept or direction—either from his father, or from any other person—but solely upon God's drawing and inclining his heart to it. That saying of Tertullian is very applicable to his prayer, "Without a monitor, because from the heart." His management of prayer with others, when advanced to eight years of age, is said to have been very remarkable, but I cannot give any particular account of that.

In the account of the remarkable conversion of the apostle Paul it is said, "Behold, he prayeth" (Acts 9:11). He no longer breathed out threatenings and slaughter against the disciples of Jesus; but earnestly prayed for mercy. Prayer is the breath of regenerate persons, and shows that they are spiritually alive; especially prayer with the spirit and with the understanding; frequent and fervent prayer, from a feeling sense of our need of spiritual blessings, such as we had no knowledge of before, nor desire after. The subjects of God's regenerating grace always cry unto him, whether they are called after a course of opposition to God, as Paul, who therefore styles himself "one born out of due time" (1 Corinthians 15:8), or in early life, as the subject of these pages.

Our blessed Lord and Saviour has said, "Suffer the little children to come unto me, and forbid them not: for of such is the kingdom of God" (Mark 10:14). Our Saviour's words here undoubtedly imply that even little children may be the subjects of divine regenerating grace, and thereby become really holy, and enjoy communion with God. If they can bear the dark impression of Adam's corrupt nature in their infancy or childhood, they may certainly be then renewed in the spirit of their mind after the image of him who created them. Almighty power and the unsearchable riches of divine grace can very easily accomplish this desirable change in children, as in the remarkable instance which is now before us.

Our young and pious convert gave afterward sufficient proof of the sincerity of his conversion, by actively promoting the cause of religion, and by acquitting himself under supernatural influence in his proper station with the spirit and temper of a real Christian. In his calling, he did abide with God.

At the proper season, he was sent to school at Canterbury, and afterward to Merchant Taylor's school in London. He continued there until his father, meeting with troubles, was obliged to remove him from these seminaries and to take him home to himself, where he gave him all instruction in the arts and languages that his circumstances would admit.

In due time he was sent to the famous University of Oxford, and became student of Christ Church there, in the year 1616, aged seventeen years, or thereabout, as Wood informs us. His industry and improvement were such that he was unanimously elected student of that house by the Dean and Canons. He resided there until he commenced Master of Arts, and a year or two after. He took the degree of Master of Arts, June 26th, in the year 1623.

Being now in some measure fitted for the work of the holy ministry, he commenced a preacher of the gospel. Wood says that he preached sometime in these parts, and afterward in Kent, at or near the place of his nativity. By the great importunity of a most intimate and affectionate friend in Norfolk, he was prevailed with to go and reside sometime with him. But he was soon called to the exercise of his ministry at Erpingham, a town in the county of Norfolk, where he continued eight or ten years. He was remarkably laborious in the work of his pastoral charge there, preaching twice every Lord's Day, expounding the Holy Scriptures, catechising the young people, and repeating in private what he had delivered in public, as several eminent ministers did in those times in England.

His mind was enlightened, and his heart animated, by a spirit of truth and of love; and he sincerely endeavoured "to divide rightly the word of truth" (2 Timothy 2:15), instructing the ignorant, arousing the careless, reproving the sinner, and comforting the saint. He attracted the esteem of many persons who readily attended him in order to enjoy the benefit of his profitable labours. And he was an eminently successful labourer in the Lord's vineyard, in the conversion of many souls.

But meeting with much trouble there, he was forced to remove from that place by Bishop Wren's extreme severity. He was summoned to the high commission-court and bailed, but before answer could be given to the articles preferred against him, the court was taken away by act of Parliament. His very intimate and affectionate friend above-mentioned, being made Warden of Manchester, took Mr. Case with him into Lancashire. Our faithful and persecuted servant of Jesus Christ was in a short time presented to a place in the neighbouring county. But great revolutions and confusions prevailing soon after in the nation, he was, by the importunity of some persons of quality, persuaded to accompany them to London.

Divine providence conducted him safely to this famous metropolis, and afterward settled him comfortably there. He was first chosen lecturer, and afterward pastor of Mary Magdalen church in Milk Street, in London. Here he was eminently laborious and faithful in his ministerial work. Beside his labours in the congregation and on the Lord's Day, he carried on a weekly lecture every Saturday, in order that the people might be better prepared for the Sabbath. And here he first set up the Morning Exercise, which was highly beneficial to many persons, and has been long continued.

The morning exercises began rather out of necessity. Many citizens of London had some near relation or friend in the army of the Earl of Essex, so many requests for prayer were sent up to the pulpit every Lord's-day for their preservation, that the minister had neither time to read them, nor to recommend their cases to God in prayer. Some divines in London therefore agreed to separate an hour for this purpose every morning, one half to be spent in prayer, and the other half in a suitable exhortation to the people.

Mr. Case began it in his church at seven o'clock in the morning, and when it had continued there a month, it was removed by turns to other churches at a distance, for the accommodation of the several parts of the city, and was called the Morning Exercise. The service was performed by different ministers, with fervent prayer both for the public welfare and for particular cases, in the presence of a large auditory. When the heat of the war was over, it became a casuistical lecture, and was carried on by the most learned and eminent divines of those times, until the restoration of King Charles the Second. Their sermons were afterward published in several volumes in quarto, under the title of the *Morning Exercises*, each sermon being the resolution of some practical case of conscience. This lecture, though in a different form, was afterward continued among the protestant dissenters.

Mr. Case's labours were not confined to his parish in Milk Street. He also carried on a lecture at Martin-in-the-Fields every Thursday, which he kept up above twenty years. Being eminently zealous for the Reformation, he was chosen a member of the Assembly of Divines at Westminster, and displayed his abilities there with success, in the service of the church. He was called frequently to preach to the members of Parliament, and on public occasions.

Mr. Case was an eminently zealous covenanter, as very clearly appears by his judicious and valuable sermons, which he preached at taking the covenant. His first sermon on this occasion was preached at Laurence Church, on the fast-day, September 27th, 1643. His second sermon was preached at Milk Street, upon Saturday evening, September 30th, for the preparation to the covenant. And his third sermon was preached on the Sabbath-day in the morning, the first of October; immediately before taking the covenant, in Milk Street church. In the preface to these three sermons he says,

> To every soul that shall enter into this holy league and covenant, my request is that they would look around them; life and death is before them; if we break with God now, we have just cause to fear; God will stand to covenant no more with us, but will avenge the quarrel with our utter destruction; if we are sincere and faithful, this covenant will be a foundation of much peace, joy, glory, and security to us and our seed, to the coming of Christ, which that it may be, shall be the earnest prayer of him, who is thy servant for Jesus' sake, Thomas Case.

He was one of those ministers who subscribed the two papers declaring against the proceedings of the Parliament in the year 1648, bringing King Charles to a trial.

He was turned out of his place of Mary Magdalen, Milk Street, for refusing the Engagement when it was vehemently urged in the time of Oliver Cromwell, or of the commonwealth after the death of King Charles the First. The oaths of allegiance and supremacy were now abolished, and a new oath was appointed, called the Engagement, which was, "To be true and faithful to the Government established without King or House of Peers." Such persons as refused this oath were declared incapable of holding any place or office of trust in the commonwealth; but as many of the excluded members of the House of Commons as would take it resumed their places. And in order to bring the Presbyterian ministers to the test, the Engagement was strongly urged, and required to be sworn and subscribed by all ministers, heads of colleges and halls, fellows of houses, graduates, and all officers in the universities. No minister was to be admitted to any ecclesiastical living, nor to be capable of enjoying any preferment in the church, unless he qualified himself by taking the Engagement within six months, publicly in the face of the congregation. Mr. Baxter says that most of the sectarian party swallowed the Engagement, and so did the king's old cavaliers, very few of them being sick of the disease of a scrupulous conscience, but the moderate Episcopal men and Presbyterians generally refused it, as Mr. Case did.

Though he was put out of his place on this account, divine providence soon opened another door for him. Christians should never despair; our heavenly Father can always provide for his children—his resources are innumerable and inexhaustible. "O fear the Lord, ye his saints: for there is no want to them who fear him" (Psalm 34:9). Mr. Case was now called to preach as lecturer, at Aldermanbury, and at Giles' Cripplegate. He continued preaching the glorious gospel of the grace of God in these congregations until he was sent prisoner to the Tower, where he was confined about six months for his concern with the celebrated Mr. Love.

Upon the death of King Charles the First, the Scots proclaimed the prince of Wales king of Scotland, and sent commissioners to the Hague, to invite him into that kingdom, if he would renounce popery and prelacy, and take the Solemn League and Covenant. The body of the English Presbyterians acted in concert with the Scots, for restoring the king upon the footing of the covenant. Several English Ministers carried on a private correspondence with the chiefs of the Scottish nation, and instead of taking the Engagement to the present powers, called them usurpers, and declined praying for them in their churches. They also declared against a general toleration, which the army and Parliament contended for. In this cause Mr. Love lost his life, and Mr. Case was imprisoned about six months under the new government, or commonwealth.

He made the best use he could of his imprisonment, falling then into the meditation which he afterward preached and printed, under the title of "Correction, Instruction." The prison-house, when persons are confined for a good cause, is not a bad school for the ministers of Christ. Some of Paul's epistles were dated there, and greatly savour of prison-supports. And we are told that Cervantes wrote his adventures of Don Quixote in a prison, and from so vigorous an exercise of all his faculties in that situation, we may conclude that a person may be in jail without being miserable.

Mr. Case, after his release, was invited to be lecturer at Giles-in-the-Fields, near London. He continued here till the king's restoration, when the former incumbent was re-admitted.

Mr. Wood says that "when the Presbyterians began to lift up their heads in the latter end of 1659, upon the generous proceedings of General Monk, he was constituted by act of Parliament, dated 14th of March that year, one of the ministers for the approbation and admission of ministers according to the Presbyterian way."

In the year 1660, he was one of the ministers deputed by his brethren in London to wait upon the king at Breda, to congratulate him on his restoration. Mr. Baxter says that the king gave them very encouraging promises of peace, and raised some of them to high expectations. He never refused them a private audience when they desired it, and to amuse them further, while they were once waiting in an anti-chamber, his majesty said his prayers with such an audible voice in the room adjoining, that the ministers might hear him: "He thanked God that he was a covenanted king; that he hoped the Lord would give him a humble, fit, forgiving, spirit; that he might have forbearance toward his offending subjects, as he expected forbearance from offended heaven." Upon hearing this, old Mr. Case lifted up his hands to heaven, and blessed God, who had given them a praying king.

In the year 1661, Mr. Case was one of the commissioners at the Savoy Conference. In the year 1662 he was ejected or silenced with his brethren by the Act of Uniformity. Wood says, "Yet ever after so long as he lives, he was not wanting to carry on the beloved cause in conventicles, for which he sometimes suffered."

In this trying season, he was chiefly concerned that divine grace might be sufficient for him (2 Corinthians 12:9) to preserve him from sin; that he might derive advantage from his crosses, and be able to say, "It is good for me that I have been afflicted" (Psalm 119:71); that he might enjoy the light of God's countenance as his support and comfort; that he might in due time come forth as gold (Job 23:10); and that he might glorify the Lord in the fires (Isaiah 14:15). And when his public ministry was at an end, he ceased not in private with the utmost diligence to do all the good he could. He preached his farewell sermon at the conclusion of his public ministry from Revelation 2:5. He says, "Christ here prescribes precious physic for the healing of this languishing church of Ephesus, compounded of three ingredients: self-reflection, holy contrition, and thorough reformation. He warmly urges these upon his hearers in order to prevent the threatened removal of their religious privileges."

In the close of the last heading, respecting the necessary reformation, "We should do something by way of extraordinary bounty and charity to the relief of God's indigent servants." He enlarges upon the pertinent passage, Daniel 4:21, and concludes thus,

> That which I would exhort you to is, for every one to set apart some considerable part of your estate, and account it as a hallowed thing, dedicated to God; as a thing which to touch were sacrilege; that you may be ready on all occasions, in all due and regular ways, to bring out for the relief of the poor. You know objects abounding in every place, and you may expect warrantable means for dispensing of what God shall put into your hands, in this manner.

This wholesome advice furnishes us with one eminently distinguishing and pleasing trait in the character of this venerable servant of Jesus Christ. God has made rich men stewards, but not proprietors. And they who have— as the gift of the living God—all things richly to enjoy, should be rich in good works, ready to distribute and willing to communicate to the poor and distressed. It is required in stewards, that a man be found faithful. And the tender care of divine providence extends to the poor as well as to the rich.

Mr. Case was eminently distinguished in his relative capacity, and praise-worthy. He had a prudent wife from the Lord; a help-meet for him. They lived together nearly forty-five years, and he often said, that "in all that time there had been no contention between them except in this, who should love one another most." They were equally yoked together, being both very pious and affectionate. They were worthy of imitation in their whole deportment. Mr. Case had no children of his own body; but his wife had children, to whom he was peculiarly attentive, and highly useful.

As soon as God had crowned his wishes, by placing him over a family, he endeavoured to glorify God as the master of a family. He now worshipped God, not only in the closet, but also in the parlour, with his wife, the children and servants in the train.

He zealously used all proper means to render the family truly religious. He was eminently attentive to the welfare of all persons who came under his roof. He instructed them carefully in the principles of religion, by helping them to understand the holy Scriptures, which were read in his family morning and evening. And his custom was to cause every child and servant to remember something that had been read. He opened these things to them in a plain and familiar manner and afterward proceeded to prayer. He mingled instruction with devotion. Many servants who lived with him, blessed God that ever they came into his house.

He died in a good old age, on the 30th of May, in the year 1682, aged eighty-four years. His life was holy, and his death was easy. He was allowed to escape, in a great degree, from the alarming approaches of the last enemy. He endured no sickness, no pain, no agonies, at the last. "The garment of mortality easily dropped off; and the servant of God fell asleep in the Lord." Rising from dinner, he desired some repose upon his bed, where as soon as he was laid, "he gathered up his feet, and so yielded up his spirit, and was gathered unto his people" (Genesis 49:33). This easy death he had much desired, and often prayed for, and he was mercifully favoured with it in answer to his prayers.

His mortal remains were decently interred in Christ Church within Newgate in London, on the 14th of June, 1682. Soon after his body was buried, a large white stone was laid over his grave; just below the steps going to the altar, with the following inscription upon it in Latin, which I shall translate into English:

> Here sweetly sleeps Thomas Case, a most faithful Minister of Jesus Christ, an excellent preacher in this city and elsewhere for many years. Educated in Christ-church, Oxford, in this church of Christ at last buried. He died 30th of May, in the year of his age 84, and in the year of our Lord, 1682.

Mr. Case lived the longest of any of those who composed the Assembly of Divines, who continued among the Dissenters. He was a man of good abilities, of sound judgment, of quick invention, of a warm spirit and steady principles; an open, plain-hearted man; an ardent and hearty lover of God and all good men; of a broken and a contrite heart, heavenly-minded and charitable. He was an excellent Scripture-preacher, an eminent man in prayer, and a very diligent and successful labourer in the Lord's vineyard.

The Reverend JAMES REID.
London, 1811.

AUTHOR'S PREFACE

Reader,

Thou hast here in the following leaves some prison thoughts, I wish I could say, experiences. If I have not written herein what I have found, I bless God, I have written what I have sought. I must humbly confess with holy Paul, "I count not myself to have apprehended"; yet through grace I can add with that blessed saint, "but this one thing I do, forgetting those things which are behind, and reaching forth unto those things which are before, I press towards the mark" (Philippians 3:13-14). God hath taught me somewhat of the doctrine, if he would please to teach me the use; God hath in some measure shown me what is to be gained by afflictions, if he would also teach me how to gain it, I should, with Moses, account my sufferings greater riches than the treasures of Egypt. The discovery is sweet; if my heart deceive me not, I would not exchange it for the wealth of both the Indies; the possession is infinitely precious. For thy advantage I have been persuaded to print; my prayers shall accompany my papers, that that God, who quickens the dead, and calls things that are not, as though they were, would please to make those broken expressions answer the aim. And for the aim's sake despise them not, but pray thou also; and when thou prayest, remember the chief of sinners, the poor and unworthy author, who, while yet in the land of the living, will be—

Thine to serve thee in the gospel of Christ,

T. CASE.

DR. MANTON'S RECOMMENDATION

To my Reverend Friend Mr. Thomas Case.

Sir,

I thank you for the favour you did me in affording me a sight of your papers; I had heard much of your notions concerning afflictions, and therefore was very thirsty till you were pleased to give me to drink of the fountain. I can now say as the queen of Sheba, "The one half was not told me"; fame came much short of state. We are perfect in no lessons so much as those into which God whips us, and cannot speak of any argument so warmly and feelingly, as when we speak out of present experience. To treat of afflictions when we ourselves flourish and abound in ease and plenty, savoureth more of the orator than the preacher, the brain than the heart. Certainly guess and imagination cannot be so good a midwife to such conceptions as sense and feeling.

It seems when you went into prison, the Spirit of God went into prison with you; and when you were shut up to others, you still lay open to the visits and free breathings of his grace. The restraints and enclosures of a prison cannot prejudice the freedom of his operations. He is a close prisoner indeed that is shut up not only from the society of men, but converse with the Holy Ghost. I begin to see there is somewhat more than a strain and reach of wit in Tertullian's consolatory discourse to the martyrs: "You went out of prison," saith he, "when you went into it, and were but sequestered from the world, that you might converse with God; the greatest prisoners and the most guilty are those that are at large, darkened with ignorance, chained with lusts, committed not by the proconsul, but God." The Lord often manifested himself to his prophets in a wilderness, and to you in your secession and retirement.

Sir, I could even envy your prison-comforts, and the sweet opportunities of a religious privacy. We that are abroad are harassed and worn out with constant public labors, and can seldom retire from the distraction of business for such free converse with God and our own souls. But we are not to choose our own portion; crosses will come soon enough without wishing for them; and if we were wise, we might make an advantage of every condition.

Good Sir, be persuaded to publish those discourses; the subject is useful, and your manner of handling it warm and affectionate; do not deprive the world of the comfort of your experiences; certainly my heart is none of the tenderest; yet if heart answereth heart I can easily foresee much success, and that you will not repent of the publication. The Lord bless your endeavours in the gospel of his dear Son. I am, Sir—

Yours in all Christian observance,

THOMAS MANTON.

CHAPTER ONE

What Lessons God Teaches by Affliction

"Blessed is the man whom thou chastenest, O LORD; and teachest him out of thy law."

Psalm 94:12

This psalm being without a title, it is not so easily determined, when, or by whom it was penned. Probably by David, when himself and the rest of the godly, were under a sore and bitter persecution by Saul, and others of the faction that bare sway under him.

Briefly, in the psalm the prophet doth these three things.

I. He doth appeal to God for vengeance on the persecutors; describing them by their pride (v.2), profaneness (vv.3-4), their intemperate virulency of speech (v.4), cruelty and bloody practices (vv.5-6), and lastly, by their atheistical security (v.7).

II. He diverteth to the enemies, endeavouring to convince them of the brutishness and folly of their atheism, the mother and nurse of the other impieties charged on them (v.8), and that by a three-fold argument:

1. The power and skill of God in creating the hearing and seeing organ in man (v.9).

2. The sovereignty of God, and the righteousness of his judgments, which he executes in the world (v.10).

3. His wisdom and knowledge, in enduing man with such an excellent intellectual faculty, whereby even the creature itself is able to attain to admirable degrees of knowledge (vv.10-11).

III. He labours to comfort the godly against all the pressures and persecutions under which they did groan and languish.

The first argument which the psalmist uses to this purpose is in the text: *the sweet fruit which is to be gathered from the bitter root of affliction.* The root indeed is bitter, but the fruit is sweet, even divine instruction; which therefore is no longer to be esteemed a punishment, but a blessing, "Blessed is the man whom thou chastenest, O Lord, and teachest him out of thy law."

This being the subject I intend to insist upon, I shall contract it into this doctrinal point of observation, namely:

The man whose *chastisements* are joined with *divine teachings* is *a blessed man*; or, *it is a blessed thing when correction and instruction go together*. The rod *and* the Word make up a complete blessing.

I shall take chastisements here in the utmost latitude, for all kinds and degrees of sufferings, whether from God, or man, or Satan; whether sufferings for sin, or sufferings for righteousness' sake. And for the doctrinal part of the point, I shall endeavour these four things:

I. To show you what those lessons are which God teaches his people by his chastisements.

II. What the nature and properties of divine teachings are.

III. In what tendency correction lies in order unto these teachings; or, what use God makes of affliction for the carrying on of the work of instruction in the hearts of his people.

IV. I shall lay down the grounds and demonstrations of the point; or considerations to evince the happiness of that man whom God is pleased to teach by his corrections.

.　　.　　.

I begin with the *lessons* which God usually teaches his people in a suffering condition. Among the many which may fall within the experience of the suffering saints, I shall observe unto you these twenty:

1. By affliction God teaches *compassion towards those who are in a suffering condition*. Truly we are very prone to be insensible of our brethren's sufferings when we ourselves are at ease in Zion. This is partly by reason of that sensuality which is in our natures, whereby we lend out our hearts so inordinately to the creature-comforts which we possess, so as to quench the tenderness and sense which we ought to have of the miseries and hardships of other men. It is also partly out of the delicacy of self-love, which makes us unwilling to sour the relish of our own sweet enjoyments with the bitter taste of strangers' afflictions. It is partly through sluggishness of spirit, which makes us unwilling to rise up from the bed of

ease and pleasure to travel in the inquiry of the state of our brethren, either abroad or at home, so that (as the apostle saith in another case) we are willingly ignorant, and are not only strangers, but are content to be strangers to their miseries and calamities.

One way or another, even Christians themselves, and such as are truly so called, are more or less guilty of the sin of the Gentiles—without natural affection, unmerciful, without tender-heartedness, without compassion.

Hence you may find that it was one of the errands upon which God sent Israel into Egypt, that, in the brick-kilns there, their hard hearts might be softened and melted into compassion towards strangers and captives. Therefore when God had turned their captivity, that was one of the first lessons of which he puts them in mind, "Thou shall not oppress a stranger" (Exodus 23:9): there is the duty, which, though negatively expressed, yet (according to the rule of interpreting the commandments) doth include all the affirmative duties of mercy and compassion: and the motive follows, "for you know the heart of a stranger" (v.9b). How did they come to know it? "Seeing ye were strangers in the land of Egypt" (v.9c). As if God had said, 'I knew thou hadst a heart of iron, and bowels of brass within thee, cruel and without compassion; and therefore I sent thee into Egypt on purpose, that by the cruelty of the Egyptians I might make your hearts tender; and that by the experience of your own sufferings and miseries you might learn—as long as you live—to lay to heart the anguish and agonies of strangers and captives; that whenever you see a stranger in your habitations, you may say, O here is a poor sojourner, an exile, I will surely have mercy upon him and show him kindness, for I myself have been a stranger and a bond-slave in Egypt.'

And upon this very account God still brings a variety of afflictions and sorrows upon his own children; he allows them to be plundered, banished, imprisoned, and reduced to great extremities, that by their own experience they may learn to draw out their souls to the hungry, and mercies towards such objects of pity that they might say within themselves, 'I know the heart of this afflicted soul, I know what it is to be plundered, to be rich one day, and the very next day to be stripped naked of all one's comforts and accommodations; I know what it is to hear poor hunger-starved children cry for bread when there is none to give them; I know what it is to be banished from dearest relations, to be like limbs torn out of the body, and to lie bleeding in their separation; I know what it is to be cast into prison, to be locked up alone in the dark, with no other company but one's own fears and sorrows. I know what it is to receive the sentence of death in one's self. Shall not I pity, and pray, and pour out my soul over such as are bleeding and languishing under the like miseries?'

And this argument makes a deeper impression when a Christian compares and measures his lighter burden of affliction with another's more grievous yoke; and reasons thus within himself, 'Imprisonment was grievous to me, and yet I enjoyed many comforts and accommodations which others did not have; I had a sweet chamber and a soft bed, when some poor members of Jesus Christ, in the Spanish inquisition and the Turkish slavery, were cast into the dungeon and sunk into the mire; their feet were hurt in the stocks, and the irons did enter into their soul. Others lie bleeding and gasping upon the cold ground with their undressed wounds, exposed to all the injuries of hunger and nakedness in the open air. I saw the face of my Christian friends sometimes, enjoyed refreshment in converse with dearest relations; while some of God's precious people were cast into dark and noisome prisons, and did not see the face of a Christian, not of a man (possibly) in five, ten, or twenty years together, unless it be of their tormenters. I had fresh diet every day, not only for necessity, but for delight, while other precious servants of God lacked their necessary bread, and lie starving in the doleful places of their sorrowful confinement. Oh! Shall not my heart yearn, and my compassions be moved within me towards such objects of misery and compassion?'

Truly, we see it daily in case of the stone, gout, strangury, and the like evils, how experience does melt the heart into tears of sympathy and fellow-feeling, while strangers to such sufferings stand wondering at, and almost deriding the heart-breaking lamentations of poor wretches. Brethren, that you may not wonder at this, I beseech you to consider what the apostle speaks of Christ himself, "It behoved him in all things to be made like unto his brethren, that he might be a merciful and faithful High Priest in things pertaining to God" (Hebrews 2:17). And again, "We have not an High Priest which cannot be touched with the feeling of our infirmities, but was in all points tempted as we are" (Hebrews 4:15).

A man would say within himself, 'Why, what need had the Lord Jesus to invest himself with a body of flesh, that he might know the infirmities of our nature, since he was God, and knew all things?' Nay, but my brethren, it seems the knowledge which Christ had as God, was different from that knowledge which he had as man; that which he had as God was intuitive; that which he had as man was experimental; experimental knowledge of misery is the heart-affecting knowledge; and therefore Christ himself would intender his own heart, as Mediator, by his own experience. And if the Lord Jesus—who was mercy itself—would put himself into a suffering condition that he might the more sweetly and affectionately act those mercies towards his suffering members, how much more do we—that by nature are uncharitable and cruel—need such practical teachings to work upon our own hearts? Certainly we cannot gain so much sense of the saints' sufferings by the most exact relation that the tongue of men or angels is able to express, no nor by all our Scripture knowledge, though sanctified, as we do by one day's experience in the school of affliction, when God is pleased to be the school-master.

2. *By chastisements God teaches us how to prize our outward mercies and comforts more, and yet to dote upon them less; to be more thankful for them, and yet less ensnared by them.* This is a mystery indeed to nature, a paradox to the world; for naturally we are very prone either to slight or to surfeit; and yet (sad to consider) we can make a shift to do both at once; we can undervalue our mercies even while we glut ourselves with them, and despise them even when we are surfeiting upon them. Witness that caution by Moses and Joshua: "When thou hast eaten and art full, take heed thou forget not the Lord thy God" (Deuteronomy 8:12,14). Behold while men fill themselves with the mercies of God, they

can neglect the God of their mercies; when God is most liberal in remembering us, we are most ungrateful to forget
him. Now therefore that we may know how to put a due
estimate upon mercies, God often cuts us short, that we may
learn to prize that by lack which our foolish unthankful
hearts slighted in the enjoyment. Thus the prodigal, who
while yet at home could despise the rich and well furnished
table of his father; when God sent him to school to the
swine-trough, could value the bread that the swine did eat.
"How many of my father's hired servants have bread
enough, and to spare!" (Luke 15:17). He would have been
glad of the reversion of broken meat that was cast into the
common basket.

I do not believe David ever slighted the ordinances, yet
certainly he never knew so well how to estimate them as
when he was banished from them. Then the remembrance of
the company of saints, the beauty of the ordinances, and the
presence of God fetched tears from his eyes and groans from
his heart, in his sorrowful exile. Oh how amiable are the as-
semblies of the saints, and the ordinances of the Sabbath,
when we are deprived of them! "In those days the word of
the Lord was precious" (1 Samuel 3:1). When was it not precious? It was always precious in the worth of it; but now it
was precious for the lack of it; prophets and prophecies were
precious, because rare; so it follows, there was no open vision. Need will teach us the worth of mercies. Our liberties
and dearest relations, how cheap and common things are
they while we possess them without any check or restraint?
While we have the keeping of our mercies in our own hands,
we make but small reckoning of them. Oh, but let God
threaten a divorce by death or banishment; let taskmasters be
set over us and our comforts, who shall measure out unto us
at their own pleasure; let us be locked up awhile under close
imprisonment, and there be kept fasting from our dearest
enjoyments; then the sight of a friend (though but through an
iron grate), the exchange of a few common civilities with a
yoke-fellow under the correction and control of a keeper,
how sweet and precious! When months and years of free enjoyments are past through, and we scarcely sit down to take
one serious view of our mercies, seldom spread them before

the Lord in prayer, or send up one thankful exclamation to God by night upon our beds; but pass by mercies as common things, scarce worth the owning, whereas in the house of bondage, in a land of captivity, the lees and dregs of those mercies will be precious, which while the vessel ran full and fresh we could hardly relish; in famine the very gleanings of our comforts are better than the whole vintage in the years of plenty.

And as God teaches us to prize our mercies, so he also teaches us moderation in the use of them while we value not to surfeit. And indeed it is the inordinate use of outward comforts which renders us unfit to prize them; we lose our esteem of mercies in excess; surfeits do usually render those things nauseous, which formerly had been our delicacies. By our excesses in creature enjoyments, reason is drowned in sense, judgment extinguished in appetite, and the affections being blunted by common exercise, even pleasures themselves become a burden.

Now this distemper God many times cures by the sharp corrosive of affliction; and by hardship teaches us moderation. Partly by inuring us to abatements and wants, whereby that which at first was necessity, afterwards grows to be our choice; hence saith the apostle, "I have learned to want" (Philippians 4:12). How? God has taught him to live off a little; by feeding us sparingly, God abates and slackens the inordinacy of the appetite. But especially, God takes off our hearts from inordinate indulgencies in a suffering condition, by discovering richer and purer satisfactions in Jesus Christ. It is God's design by withdrawing the creature, to fix the soul upon himself; the voice of the rod is, "O taste and see how good the Lord is" (Psalm 34:8); which when the soul hath once perceived, thrusting the creature away with contempt and indignation, it opens itself to God, saying, "Whom have I in heaven, but thee? And there is none upon earth that I desire in comparison of thee" (Psalm 73:25). Surely it was in the school of affliction that David learned that lesson, even when the wicked prospered, and himself, with the rest of the godly, "were plagued all the day long, and chastened every morning" (Psalm 73:14).

3. *God teaches self-denial and obedient submission to the will of God by his chastisements.*

In our prosperity we are full of our own wills, and usually we give God counsel when he looks for obedience; and so we dispute our cross when we should take it up; but now by bearing a little we learn to bear more; the trial of our faith works patience; the more we suffer, the more God fits us for suffering:

a.) *By working us off from our own wills,* "Folly is bound up in the heart of (God's) children; but the rod if correction driveth it from them" (Proverbs 22:15).

b.) *By inuring us to the cross.* The bullock which is unaccustomed to the yoke, is very impatient under the hand of the farmer; but after it is inured to labour, it willingly puts its neck under the yoke. And so it is with Christians; after a while the yoke of affliction begins to be well settled, and by bearing much we learn to bear with quietness: a new cart makes a great noise and squeaking, but when once used, it goes silently under the greatest load. None murmur so much at sufferings as they who have suffered least; whereas on the contrary, we see many times that they who have the heaviest burden upon their backs are most patient. "He sitteth alone, and keepeth silence, because he hath borne it upon him" (Lamentations 3:28); in other words, he is patient because he is acquainted with sorrows. When people cry out, 'Oh, never such sufferings as mine!' it is an argument they are strangers to afflictions.

c.) *Because by chastisements God works out by degrees the delicacy of spirit which we contract in our prosperity.* Prosperity makes us tender; they who are always kept in the warm house, dare not put their head out of doors in a storm. None are so unfit for sufferings as they that have been always dandled upon the knee of providence; the most delicate constitutions are most unfit for hardship.

d.) Lastly and chiefly, this comes to pass because *by sufferings we come to taste the fruit of sufferings.* "No chastening for the present seems joyous, but grievous; but afterwards it yields the peaceable fruits of righteousness unto them which are exercised thereby" (Hebrews 12:11).

Thus, one way or another, God works his children into a sweet obedient frame by their sufferings. It is even said of Christ himself, "He learned obedience by the thing which he suffered" (Hebrews 5:8). By his own experience he came to know what it was to be subject to the will of his Father. It is equally true of adopted children, they learn obedience by the things which they suffer; and that not only in a passive, but in an active sense. By suffering God's will we learn to do God's will: God hath no such obedient children as those whom he nurtures in the school of affliction. At length God brings all his scholars to subscribe, *what* God will, *when* God will, *how* God will: "Thy will be done on earth as it is in heaven" (Matthew 6:10). A blessed lesson.

4. *God teaches humility and meekness of spirit by affliction.* It is one of God's designs in affliction to hide pride from man; to spread sackcloth upon all his glory, so that man may see no excellency (wherein to pride himself) in all the creature. God led Israel forty years in the wilderness to humble them. By the thorns of the wilderness God pricked the bladder of pride, and let out the windiness of self-opinion which was in their hearts. Prosperity usually makes men surly and supercilious towards their poor brethren. The rich man answers roughly even while the poor man uses entreaties and makes his addresses to him with all humility and observance. He holds up his head or turns his back upon him with scorn and contempt, and thinks himself too good to give his poor neighbour a soft and peaceable answer. Pride is a disposition which naturally runs in our veins, and it is nourished by ease and prosperity. And therefore, to tame this pride of spirit that is in man, God takes him into the house of correction, puts his feet in the stocks and there teaches him to know himself. "He humbled thee, and suffered thee to hunger" (Deuteronomy 8:3); hunger brought down Israel's stomach, and did eat out that proud flesh which began to rankle. Hence it is, that if you take the children of God either yet in, or newly come out of, the furnace of affliction, you shall observe them to be the humblest, meekest creatures upon the earth; as it is said, "A little child may lead them" (Isaiah 11:6), whereas before it may be they were so stiff and high, that an angel of God could not tell how to deal with

them; now the lowest of God's servants may reprove and counsel them. That David, who put his poor Ammonite prisoners and captives to death in cold blood (2 Samuel 12:31), banishment and persecution made so tame that not only the righteous might reprove him; but even the wicked might reproach him, yet he holds his peace; or if he speaks, it is in words of patience and submission: "So let him curse, because the Lord hath said, 'Curse David'" (2 Samuel 16). A man by trouble comes to know his own heart, which in prosperity he was a stranger to. He sees the weakness of his grace and the strength of his corruption; how nothing is weak but grace, nothing strong but sin; and this lays him in the dust. "Oh wretch that I am!" (Romans 7:24). And truly when a man has learned this lesson he is not far from deliverance; "Seek the Lord all ye meek of the earth, seek righteousness; seek meekness, it may be ye shall be hid in the day of the Lord's anger" (Zephaniah 2:3). This is God's design, first, to humble his people by affliction, and then to save them from it. "For the Lord taketh pleasure in his people, he will beautify the meek with salvation" (Psalm 149:4).

5. *By affliction God discovers unknown corruption in the hearts of his people.* He led thee through the wilderness these forty years "to humble thee, and to prove thee, to know what was in thy heart" (Deuteronomy 8:2); in other words, to make thee know what was in thy heart: what pride, what impatience, what unbelief, what idolatry, what distrust of God, what murmuring, what unthankfulness was in thy heart—and thou didst never notice it. Sin lieth very close and deep, and is not easily discerned, till the fire of affliction comes and makes a separation of the precious from the vile. 'What shall I do,' saith God, 'for the daughter of my people? They are exceeding bad, and they know it not. What shall I do with them? I will melt them and try them. Into the furnace they shall go, and there I will show them what is in their hearts.' In the furnace we see more corruption than ever appeared before, or was suspected. 'Oh,' saith the poor soul whom God hath taught in the school of affliction, 'I never thought my heart so bad as now I see it is. I could not have believed the world had had so much interest in my heart, and Christ so little. I did not think my faith had been so weak

and my fears so strong. I find that faith weak in danger, which I thought had been strong out of danger. Little did I think the sight of death would have been so terrible, parting with nearest friends and dearest relations so piercing. Oh how unskillful and unwise am I to manage a suffering condition, to discern God's ends, to find out what God would have me to do, to moderate the violences of my own passions, to apply the counsels and comforts of the Word for their proper ends and uses! Oh where is my patience, my love, my zeal, my rejoicing in tribulation? Ah, did I ever think to find my heart so discomposed, my affections so out of command, my graces so to seek when I should fall into diverse temptations? What a great deal of self-love, pride, distrust in God, creature confidence, discontent, murmuring, rising of heart against the holy and righteous dispensations of God! Is there boiling and fretting within me? Woe is me, what a heart have I!'

And besides all this, in the hour of temptation God brings old sins to remembrance. "We are verily guilty concerning our brother" (Genesis 42:21), could Joseph's brethren say twenty years after they had sold him for a slave, when they were in danger to be questioned for their lives, as they supposed; and thus when the Israelites cry to God in their sore distress for rescue and deliverance, God puts them in mind of their old apostasies: "Ye have forsaken me, and served other gods. Go, and cry to the gods whom ye have chosen" (Judges 10:13-14). Suffering times are times of bringing to mind sin. "If they bethink themselves in the land whither they were carried captives" (2 Chronicles 6:37), if they bring back to heart—captivity is a time of turning in upon ourselves, and bringing back to heart our doings which have not been good in God's sight. Thus David under the rod could call himself to account; "I thought on my ways, and turned my feet unto thy testimonies" (Psalm 119:59).

6. *In the school of affliction God teaches us to pray.* They that never prayed before, will pray in affliction. "Lord, in trouble they have visited thee: they poured out a prayer when thy chastening was upon them" (Isaiah 26:16). They that kept their distance with God before, yea, that said to the Almighty 'depart from us,' in their affliction can bestow a visit

upon God; in trouble they have visited thee, and they that never prayed before, or at least did but now and then drop out a sleepy sluggish wish, can now pour out a prayer when chastisement is upon their loins. Rebels, fools, mariners, even the worst of men, can cry to God in their trouble. The very heathen mariners fall to their prayers in a storm, and can awaken the sleepy prophet to this duty, "What meanest thou, O sleeper! Arise and call upon thy God" (Jonah 1:6). Hence we used to say, "He that cannot pray, let him go to sea."

Thus, I say, affliction opens dumb lips, and unties the strings of the tongue to call upon God. And those whom God teaches in affliction learn to pray in another manner—more frequently, more fervently.

More frequently. God's people are vessels full of the spirit of prayer, and affliction is a piercer, whereby God draws it out. "For my love they are my adversaries, but I give myself unto prayer" (Psalm 109:4). David was always a praying man, but now under persecution he did nothing else, "I give myself unto prayer"; as wicked men give themselves up to their wickedness, so David gave himself up to prayer, he made it his work. Hence you may observe that all the psalms are almost nothing else but the runnings out of David's spirit in prayer under a variety of afflictions and persecutions. As his troubles were multiplied, so his prayers did multiply. The holy man was never in that condition wherein he could not pray. Alas, it is sad to consider, that in our peace and tranquility, we pray by fits and starts many times; we suffer every trifle to come and justle out prayer; but in affliction God keeps us upon our knees, and as it were "tieth the sacrifice to the horns of the altar" (Psalm 118:27).

More fervently. As he teaches us to pray more frequently, so also to pray more fervently. It is said even of Christ himself, that "being in an agony he prayed more earnestly" (Luke 22:44), more intensely; he prayed till he sweat, yea till he sweat great drops of blood; the reason being because he had not only the pangs of death, but also the sense of his Father's wrath to dread. So it is with believers many times. Outward afflictions are accompanied with inward desertions.

Truly Christians, those prayers which you contented yourselves with in the day of your peace and prosperity, will not serve your turn in the hour of temptation, when you will call to mind your short, slight, cold, dead, sleepy, formal devotions in your families and closets, and be ashamed of them. Then you will see need of praying over all your prayers again, and stir up yourselves to take hold on God. Indeed for this very end God sends his people into captivity, that he may draw out the spirit of prayer, which they have suffered to lie dead within them. "O my dove that art in the clefts of the rock, in the secret places of the stairs; let me see thy countenance, let me hear thy voice; for sweet is thy voice, and thy countenance is comely" (Song of Solomon 2:14).

Christ's dove never looks more beautiful in his eyes than when her cheeks are bedewed with tears. Nor does she ever make sweeter music in his ears than when she mourns to him out of the rock and from under the stairs, in a dark and desolate condition. Then, saith Christ, "Thy countenance is comely, and sweet is thy voice."

7. *By correction God brings the children of promise into more acquaintance with the Word.* "It is good for me that I have been afflicted, that I might learn thy statutes" (Psalm 119:71). God sent David into the school of affliction to learn his statutes there.

By correction the people of God learn: a.) to converse with the Word of God more abundantly, b.) to understand it more clearly, and c.) to relish it more sweetly.

a.) *By affliction we come to converse with the Word more abundantly.* It is our duty at all times to study the Word, to "let it dwell richly in us in all wisdom" (Colossians 3:16). Job "esteemed the words of God's mouth more than his necessary food" (Job 23:12). It is our happiness as well as our duty. Blessed is the man that walks not in the counsel of the ungodly, "but his delight is in the law of the Lord, and in his law doth he meditate day and night" (Psalm 1:2).

But through distraction without and distemper within, the children of God many times grow strangers to their Bibles; we suffer diversions to interpose between the Word and our hearts, and therefore God deals with us as we do with our children, we whip them to their books by the rod of correction. "Princes did sit and speak against me" (Psalm 119:23a), says David, in other words, they sat in council to take away his life, that they might condemn him as a traitor against Saul. And what did he in the meantime? It follows, "but thy servant did meditate in thy statutes" (v.23b). And again, "Princes have persecuted me without a cause, but my heart standeth in awe of thy Word" (Psalm 119:161). While the persecutors are consulting with the oracles of hell to sin against David, he is consulting with the oracles of heaven, that he might not sin against God; while they sinned and feared not, David feared and sinned not.

b.) *By affliction we learn to understand the Word more clearly.* As it was with the disciples in reference to Christ's resurrection, "These things understood not his disciples at the first, but when Jesus was glorified, then remembered they these things" (John 12:16). So it is with the people of God many times in reference to affliction—the rod expounds the Word, providence interprets the promise. We would never understand some Scriptures, had God not sent us into the school of affliction. Then we can remember how it is written: we can bring God's Word and his works together.

c.) *Affliction makes us relish the Word more sweetly.* In prosperity many times we suffer the luscious enjoyments of the world so to distemper our palates that we cannot relish the Word, nor taste any more sweetness in it than in the white of an egg, as Job speaks in another case (Job 6:6).

But when God hath kept us for weeks, months, and years it may be, fasting from the world's dainties; when we are thoroughly hungerbitten in the creature, then "How sweet are thy words to my taste! Sweeter than honey to my mouth!" (Psalm 119:103)—these are the words which David spoke in his affliction. The rod did sweeten the Word: 'It is my delight, my joy, a nest of sweetnesses.' "The full soul loathes the honey-comb"; when we are crammed with creature comforts, we nauseate many times the very Word itself; "but to the hungry soul every bitter thing is sweet" (Proverbs 27:7). Let God famish the world round about us, then how cordial is a word of Scripture consolation! How precious are the promises! "Oh," said a gracious woman reduced to great straits, "I have made many a meal's meat upon the promises when I have wanted bread." The Word is never so sweet as when the world is most bitter; and therefore God doth lay mustard upon the teats of the world, that we might go to the breasts of the Word, and there "suck and be satisfied with the milk of consolation" (Isaiah 66:11). "This is my comfort in my affliction, for thy Word hath quickened me" (Psalm 119:50). Blessed be God for that correction which sweetens the Word unto us.

8. *God, by bringing his people into troubles, especially if life-threatening dangers, shows them the necessity of sound evidence for heaven and happiness.*

Alas, with what easy and slight evidences do we often content ourselves in the time of our prosperity, when the candle of the Almighty doth shine in our tabernacles, when all is peace and quiet round about us! The heart being taken up with other fruitions, we lack both the time and will to pursue the trial of our own estates. People mind only what will serve their turn for the present and quiet their hearts so that they may follow their pleasures and profits with the less regret. Therefore to save themselves a labour, they take that for evidence which the sluggish carnal heart wishes were so. But now in the hour of temptation, fig-leaves will cover nakedness no longer; nothing will serve the turn but what will be able to stand before God, and endure the trial of fire in the day of Christ.

O, then one clear and unquestionable evidence of interest in Christ, and the love of God, will be worth ten thousand worlds; shadows and appearances of grace will vanish before the Searcher of Hearts. It must be perfect love that will cast out fear (1 John 4:18); only truth and soundness of grace can give boldness in the day of judgment. Ah, what idle and deceitful hearts are in us, that can take up with loose conjectures, yet go to the Word and sacrament with these evidences, and still dare not venture to die upon them? And yet good and upright is the Lord that will teach sinners his way, that by the thunderclaps of his righteous judgments will awaken the vain creature out of these foolish dreams in which if they should die, they were undone forever. Well, let us be still urging and pressing these questions upon our souls—'Will this faith save me when I come to stand before the throne of the Lamb? Will this love give me boldness in the day of judgment? Will this evidence serve my turn when I come to die?' O Christians, let us be afraid to lie down with that evidence in our beds, wherewith we dare not lie down in our graves.

9. *In the time of our trouble God causes us to see what an evil and bitter thing it is to grieve his good Spirit.*

When we are in the bitterness of our spirits, and want the Comforter, then we begin to call to mind how often we have grieved the Spirit which would have been a Comforter to us and have sealed us to the day of redemption (Ephesians 4:30); and say within ourselves in reference to the Spirit of God, as once the sons of Jacob said one to another in reference to Joseph, "We are verily guilty concerning our brother, in that we saw the anguish of his soul, when he besought us, and we would not hear; therefore is this distress come upon us" (Genesis 42:21). In some such language, I say, will the soul in the hour of temptation bespeak itself. Ah, I am verily guilty concerning that tender Spirit of Grace and Comfort which hath often said, "O! Do not this abominable thing which I hate" (Jeremiah 44:4); but I would not hear. Is not this he whose rebukes I have slighted, whose counsels I have despised, whose warnings I have neglected, yea whose comforts I have undervalued, and counted them as a small thing? Ah wretch! How just is it now that the Spirit of God should withdraw? That he should despise my sorrows, and laugh at my tears; shut out my prayers, quench my smoking flax, and break my bruised reed (cf. Isaiah 42:3)? Well, if the Lord shall indeed be pleased to bring my soul out of trouble, and to revive my fainting spirit with his sweet consolations, I hope I shall carry myself for the future more obedient to the counsels and rebukes of the Spirit of Grace.

10. *By chastisements God draws the soul into sweet and near communion with himself.* Outward prosperity is a great obstruction to our communion with God; partly because by letting out our affections inordinately to the creature, we suffer the world to come between God and our hearts, and so intercept that sweet and constant traffic and intercourse which should be between God and us. God's people offend most in their lawful comforts because there the snare being

not so visible as in grosser sins, they are the easier taken; we are soonest surprised where we are least jealous.

Outward prosperity also obstructs our communion with God because we fail to keep watch against lesser sins. While our hearts are warmed with prosperity, we think many times small sins can do no great harm; but in this we woefully deceive ourselves, for besides that the least sin hath the nature of sin it, as the least drop of poison is poison; and that in smaller sins there is the greater contempt of God, inasmuch as we stand out with God for a trifle as we count it, and venture his displeasure for a little sensual satisfaction.

I say, besides these and many other considerations which may render our small sins great provocations, this is one unspeakable mischief, that small sins interrupt our communion with God as much as great sins, and sometimes more. For whereas great sins, by making deep wounds upon conscience, make the soul go bleeding to the throne of grace, and there to mourn and lament, and never to give God rest till he gives rest to the soul, and by a fresh sprinkling of the blood of Christ, to recover peace and communion with God—smaller sins, not impressing such horror upon the conscience, are swallowed in silence with less regret, and so do insensibly alienate and estrange the heart from Jesus Christ. The least hair casts its shadow; a barley corn laid upon the sight of the eye keeps out the light of the sun as well as a mountain. The eye of the soul must be kept very clear that will see God: "Blessed are the pure in heart, for they shall see God" (Matthew 5:8). Little sins, though they do not disturb reason so much as great sins, yet they defile conscience, and the conscience under defilement (unlamented) is shy of God, and God shy of it.

But affliction sanctifies; as it deadens the heart to the world, so it awakens and softens the conscience against sin; the soul is made sensible of her departure from God, and of the bitter fruits of that departure, and now begins to lament after God in Augustine's language, "Lord, thou hast made my heart for thyself, and it is restless and unquiet till it can rest in thee."

The soul hath many turnings and windings, but like Noah's dove, it can find no place for its foot to rest on till it return into the ark from whence it came; and when the soul hath been weather-beaten abroad, if God is pleased to put forth his hand and take it into himself when dearest relations are become strangers (as David complains), if God comes and gives the soul a visit when the poor creature is in darkness and can see no light, then for God to lift up the light of his countenance and shine with a gracious smile upon the soul, and say unto it, "I am thy salvation" (Psalm 35:3); of what sweet and unspeakable refreshment and consolation is this to the afflicted spirit? And what a gracious condescension is this in God, that when the soul by prosperity hath "waxed wanton against Christ" (1 Timothy 5:11), and sported itself in unspouselike familiarities with strangers, Jesus Christ should send it into the house of correction, and there by the discipline of the rod, correct and work out the wantonness of the flesh. And when he hath made it fit for his presence, he takes it into sweet and social communion with himself again! This is astonishing mercy and goodness that cannot be paralleled in the whole creation!

11. *God makes affliction the exercise and improvement of grace.* In prosperity grace many times lies dead in the soul, which affliction awakens and draws forth into exercise; the winter of our outward comforts proves not seldom the spring of our graces; frost and snow starve the weed, but nourish the good corn. Though faith and patience are of a universal influence in a holy life, yet affliction gives them their perfect work.

Of the times of persecution it is said, "Here is the patience and faith of the saints" (Revelation 14:12); that is, now is the time for the saints of God to exert their faith and patience, and to let them have their perfect work. There is a work of patience, and there is a perfect work, "the trial of faith worketh patience" (James 1:3). It works, or as the word κατεργάζεται signifies, it *perfects*. The cross exercises, and exercise perfects the grace of patience: as sufferings arise, so patience arises also, "Be patient, brethren, till the coming of the Lord" (James 5:7): in other words, bear the affliction till Christ comes and takes it off. Let your patience be of the same extent with your sufferings. As patience, so faith is not acted only, but perfected by temptations. Sometimes the soul finds its faith lively in a suffering condition, which before it questioned whether it were alive or no; or if affliction does not find it lively, it *makes* it lively. In the same furnace of affliction wherein God tries our faith he doth refine it, and purifies it more and more from the dross of infidelity.

They are the purest acts of faith which the soul puts forth in the dark; faith never believes more than when it cannot see, because then the soul hath nothing to stay itself upon but God. Sense, while it seems to help, renders the work of faith more difficult by doubling it; a man must first believe the insufficiency of what he sees before he can believe the all-sufficiency of him that is invisible, "We look not at the things which are seen, but at the things which are not seen" (2 Corinthians 4:18).

It is harder to live by faith in abundance than in need. The soul is a step nearer living upon God when it hath nothing to live upon but God; yea, and when God is not seen, he is most believed. "My God, my God, why hast thou forsaken me?" (Matthew 27:46). Observe, and you shall find a great deal more of precious faith in that desertion than of complaint; faith breaks forth first, 'My God,' before 'forsaken': you have two words of faith for one of despair, "My God, my God, why hast thou forsaken me?" Faith speaks twice before sense can speak once. Again, faith speaks confidently and positively, thou art 'my God'; sense speaks dubiously, 'why hast thou?' as if sense durst not call it a forsaking while faith dares say, 'my God.' Surely faith is never so much faith as in desertion. Faith's triumphs lie in the midst of despair, and even in this sense also, "Having not seen, yet believing, we rejoice with joy unspeakable and full of glory" (1 Peter 1:8).

Godly sorrow, how it is enlarged by sanctified affliction! That stream which was accustomed to run in the channel of worldly crosses now is diverted into the channel of sin: "I will bear the indignation of the Lord, because I have sinned" (Micah 7:9). Any burden is light in comparison of sin, the very indignation of God. The soul that God teaches by his chastisements can stand under the burden of God's indignation for sin when it cannot stand under sin which hath kindled that indignation. 'Ah,' crieth Job upon the dunghill, "I have sinned, what shall I do unto thee, O thou preserver of men?" (Job 7:20). He forgets his suffering in his sin; he saith not, 'I have lost all my substance. I am now upon the dung-hill as naked as ever I was born, save that I am clothed with scabs. My friends reproach me, my wife curses me, or that which is worse, she bids me curse God. Satan persecutes me, and God himself has become my enemy. All this is befallen me; what wilt thou do unto me, O thou preserver of men?' But instead it is, "I have sinned, what shall I do unto thee?" Sufferings convict of sin, and the sense of sin swallows up the sense of sufferings.

And what shall I say more? The time would fail to instance in other graces, love, fear, holiness, and so forth. "By this shall the iniquity of Jacob be purged, and this is all the fruit to take away his sin" (Isaiah 27:9).

Grace is never more grace than when besieged with temptations. The battle draws forth that fortitude and bravery which in time of peace lay chilled in the veins for lack of opposition and exercise. Tribulation worketh patience.

12. *The necessity and excellency of the life of faith is learned in the school of affliction.*

a.) The necessity of living by faith. Where sense ends, faith begins; the vision is for an appointed time, but what shall we do in the meantime? "The just shall live by faith" (2 Corinthians 5:7); live by faith, or die in despair. When God pulls away the bull-rushes of creature supports, the soul must either swim or sink. God teaches this lesson—

[1.] By the uncertainty of second causes, and the vicissitudes that are in creature expectations. A little hope today, tomorrow reduced to despair; good news today, Pharaoh says Israel shall go; bad news tomorrow, he rages, and swears that "if Moses see his face any more he shall surely die" (Exodus 10:28).

O the ebbs and flows of sublunary hopes! One speaks a word of comfort, another words of terror; now a parcel of good words, and shortly thereafter a threatening. The sick man is in hopes of reviving today, but tomorrow at the point of death. What a woeful heart-dividing life is a life of sense, a life that is worse than death itself; to be thus bandied up and down between hopes and fears; to be baffled to and fro between the maybe's of second causes! To be like mariners upon the billows and surges of the tempestuous sea! "They mount up to heaven, they go down again to the depths; their soul is melted because of trouble; they reel to and fro and stagger like a drunken man, and are at their wits' end" (Psalm 107:26-27).

[2.] By the disappointment of the creature. How often does the creature totally fail and abuse our expectation! Like the deceitful brook, to which Job most elegantly compares his brethren, which mocks the traveler who comes for a draught of water to quench his thirst, but is sent away with confusion and shame. "Surely men of low degree are vanity, and men of high degree are a lie" (Psalm 62:9): Men of low degree would help, but cannot—there is vanity; and men of high degree can help many times, but will not; no, not when they have promised and sworn—there is a lie: both disappoint, the one by the necessity, the other by deceit; and disappointment is one of the greatest torments that a rational creature is capable of. David himself "looked on his right hand, and beheld, and there was no man that would know him" (Psalm 142:4). Peter-like, they "knew not the man" (Matthew 26:72); they made as if they had never seen him before. So that churl Nabal, "Who is David? And who is the son of Jesse?" (1 Samuel 25:10). And it was not Nabal only that stood at this distance from him, his nearest and dearest acquaintance cast him off: "Lover and friend hast thou put far from me, and mine acquaintance into darkness" (Psalm 88:18). "Refuge failed me, no man cared for my soul" (Psalm 142:4).

St. Paul was in no better condition in the persecution which befell him at Rome, "At my first answer no man stood with me, but all men forsook me" (2 Timothy 4:16). There was not a man of all them that sat under the famous apostle's ministry that would dare appear to speak a word for him, or to him. Oh bitter disappointment, had not he had faith to support him under it! Sorrow and shame are the fruits of creature-expectation.

But now on the contrary, "They looked unto the Lord and were enlightened, and their faces were not ashamed" (Psalm 34:5). Faith meets with no disappointment, God is always better than our expectation, "Nevertheless the Lord stood with me, and strengthened me—and I was delivered from the mouth of the lion" (2 Timothy 4:17). By such experiences do we learn the necessity of living by faith, "I had perished in my affliction, unless thy law had been my delight" (Psalm 119:92). Unless David had learned to live by a promise, he would have been a dead man.

Surely he dieth oft whose life is bound up in the dying creature. As often as the creature fails, his hope fails and his heart fails. When the creature dies, his hope gives up the ghost. He only lives an unchangeable life, that by faith can live upon an unchangeable God.

We hear such things indeed in the Word; but we believe them not till our own experience convinces us of our infidelity. A long time do we stick totally in the creature, knowing no other life than that of sense and reason, "sacrificing to our own nets, and burning incense to our own drag" (Habakkuk 1:16).

And because the Word tells us much of living by faith, we would eagerly patch up a life between faith and sense, which indeed is not a life of faith. Though we may use means, we must trust God and trust him solely; and therefore to bring us to this, God allows us to be tried and vexed with the mockery of second causes, and when we have spent all upon these physicians of no value, then, and never till then, we resolve for Christ.

When David had experienced sufficiently the falseness and hypocrisy of Saul and his parasites, "They delight in lies, they bless with their mouth, but they curse inwardly," then he resolves never to trust a creature more: "My soul wait thou only upon God, he only is my Rock and my salvation" (Psalm 62:4-6).

Unmixed trust in God is the fruit of our experience of the creature's vanity. We never resolve exclusively for God, till with the prodigal, we are whipped home naked to our father's house. When the Church had run herself barefoot in following her lovers, who answered her expectation with nothing but fear, and sent her away with shame instead of glory; then she can go home, and confessing her atheism and folly, gives up herself purely to divine protection: "Ashur shall not save us, we will not ride upon horses, neither will we say any more to the work of our hands, 'Ye are our gods'; for in thee the fatherless findeth mercy" (Hosea 14:3).

b.) *By the mutability and disappointment of the creature, God teaches his people the excellency of the life of faith.* David, when he learns it in the school of affliction, publishes it for the use and benefit of after ages. "Happy is he that hath the God of Jacob for his help, whose hope is in the Lord his God" (Psalm 146:5). He had before entered a caveat against creature confidence, "Put not your trust in princes, nor in the son of man"; and gives the reason of it, there is no help or salvation in the best of men—"nor in the son of man, in whom there is no help" (v.3).

Alas, he is but a little breathing clay; and when that breath goeth forth, he returns to his earth. When the breath is gone, there is nothing but a little lump of clay remaining. In that very day his thoughts perish; when the man dieth all his counsels and plots and projects die with him; and having thus put in his caution against creature dependence, and given in the account of the vanity thereof, he shows the difference between trust in a dying man and a living God.

Only trust in God is able to make a man happy. Those who have the great men of the world to trust in may seem happy, but only he who hath the God of heaven to trust is happy, "Blessed is he who hath the God of Jacob for his help." Why so? Because while they that trust in princes shall be disappointed, he that trusts in God shall never be disappointed; for he is Jehovah: whose hope is in the Lord, or in Jehovah, his God: "He made heaven and earth, the sea, and all that therein is" (v.6); and he that gave being to every creature can give being to his promise also. Can anything be too hard for a creating God? And as he can, so he will, for he keepeth truth forever, heaven and earth may pass away, but not one jot or tittle of his promise shall pass away till all be fulfilled (Matthew 5:18).

Men may prove unfaithful, but God will never prove unfaithful; he keepeth truth forever, "Faithful is he that hath promised" (Hebrews 10:23). And thus the soul comes to see the sweetness and excellence of a life of faith while others are mocked, abused, and slain, by disappointment from the second causes, "He is kept in perfect peace, whose mind is stayed on God, because he trusteth in him" (Isaiah 26:3): he liveth indeed, that liveth in him to whom *always* is essential.

The excellency of a life of faith discovers itself in these four particulars—It is a secure life, a sweet life, an easy life, and an honourable life.

[1.] *The life of faith is a secure life.* "He shall dwell on high, his place of defence shall be the munition of rocks" (Isaiah 33:16). How securely doth he dwell, whose fortifications are impregnable, inaccessible rocks? In the Hebrew it is, "He shall dwell in heights," or "in high places, munition of rocks"; or rocks so high that none can scale them, rocks so thick that no breach can be made in them, rocks within rocks, "munition of rocks"; and rocks so deep that none can undermine them. Surely a person thus defended on every side need not fear storming.

Objection. Aye, though rocks may be a good fence, they are but ill food, a man cannot feed on rocks; rocky places are barren, though impregnable; he may be starved, though he cannot be stormed!

Answer. No! The words following relieve that fear also, "Bread shall be given him" (v.16). He shall have bread enough, and it shall cost him nothing—it shall be given to him.

And whereas a rock is but a dry situation, without either springs or streams, and thereupon a man might be exposed to perishing for lack of water. Thirst will slay as well as hunger. Therefore it is likewise added, "His water shall be sure" (v.16). He shall have waters which neither summer's heat nor winter's frosts shall be able to dry up, never-failing waters shall fill his cisterns from day to day; "His waters shall be sure."

Under such an excellent metaphor is the security of a life of faith described, and this metaphor is expounded in another place, "Salvation will God appoint for walls and bulwarks" (Isaiah 26:1). Walls and bulwarks shall not be their salvation, but salvation their walls and bulwarks. How safely do they dwell who are walled about with salvation itself? The bulwarks are salvation, and that salvation is Jehovah; for so it follows, "Trust ye in the Lord forever, for in the Lord Jehovah is everlasting strength" (v.4). The Lord Jeho-

vah is the rock of all ages: his place of defence is the ammu-
nition of rocks; and the Lord Jehovah is those rocks, a rock
of ages. Ages pass away, one after another, but the rock
abides, and abides forever; "In the Lord Jehovah is everlasting strength" (v.4).

He that rained manna in the wilderness will give bread,
and he that fetched water out of the rock will be a never-
failing fountain; his waters shall be sure.

[2.] *The life of faith is sweet.* Is it not a sweet thing to
fetch all our waters from the fountain, from the spring-head,
before they be degenerated or muddied by the miry channel?
Faith says to God, "All my fresh springs art in thee" (Psalm
87:7). Is it not sweet to be fixed and composed in the midst
of all the mutations and confusions that are under the sun?
This is the privilege of him that liveth by faith, "No evil tid-
ings shall make him afraid, his heart is fixed, trusting in the
Lord" (Psalm 112:7). And again, "Thou wilt keep him in
perfect peace whose mind is stayed on thee, because he
trusteth in thee" (Isaiah 26:3). The Hebrew has it "peace,
peace"; that is, multiplied peace; pure, unmixed peace. Constant and everlasting peace is the portion of him that lives by
faith, so far as he lives by faith. Unless sense and reason
break into disquiet, he lives in a most sweet and immutable
serenity.

[3.] *The life of faith is an easy life.* It is an easy life to have
all provisions brought in to a man without any care or trouble. Such is the privilege of a believer; he hath a *quietus est*, a
supersedeas from all his cares. "In nothing be careful, but in
everything by prayer and supplication, with thanksgiving, let
your requests be made known to God" (Philippians 4:6).
Faith leaves a believer nothing to do but to pray and give
thanks: to pray for what he wants, and to give thanks for
what he has; that is all he hath to do.

It is true, believers must labour and travel in the use of
means, as well as the rest of the sons of Adam, but it is without care, without anxious, heart-dividing, soul-distracting
care. O that is the thorn, the sting which the sin of man and
the curse of God hath thrust into all our labours: care and
distraction; and faith pulls this out, so now all the labour of
faith is an easy labour, like the labour of Adam in paradise.

Faith uses means but trusts God; obediently closes with the providence of means but sweetly leaves the providence of success to God. Yea, faith can trust God when there are no means to use, and say; "Although the fig-tree shall not blossom, neither shall fruit be in the vines; the labour of the olive shall fail, and the field shall yield no meat; the flock shall be cut off from the fold, and there shall be no herd in the stall; yet I will rejoice in the Lord, I will joy in the God of my salvation" (Habakkuk 3:17-18).

Faith can live upon God when there is a famine upon the whole creation. The peace of God is as a court of guard, to fence the heart from all surprises of fear and trouble, "In nothing be careful, but in every thing pray and give thanks, and the peace of God which passeth all understanding shall keep your hearts and minds through Christ Jesus" (Philippians 4:6-7). As faith enjoys God in all things in the greatest abundance, so she can enjoy all things in God in the deepest want.

[4.] *The life of faith is an honourable life.* It is the honour of the favourite that he can go immediately to his prince, when strangers must follow the procedures of court accesses. Yea, without all peradventure, it is an honourable life to live as God himself lives; and this is the glory of God, that he lives in himself and of himself; and truly in their proportion, such honour have all his saints; they live in God and upon God here by faith; and they shall live in God and upon God hereafter by sight, in the beatific vision. The saints have a self-sufficiency (as it were) within themselves (Proverbs 14:14).

This is the excellency of the life of faith, and this the people of God experience by their sufferings, whereby God calls them out of the world, and taking them into himself, he doth reveal to them by degree the mystery and privilege of living upon God, and upon God alone.

13. *By afflictions and distresses God takes us off from self-confidence, and teaches us to trust him more, and ourselves less.*

This is the same with the former, save only that we speak now of trust in God, in opposition to confidence in ourselves, and not in others; a distemper that prevails much in our natures: ever since we rendered ourselves able to do nothing, nothing but sin, we think ourselves able to do anything; we fancy to ourselves a kind of omnipotence, when all our strength is to sit still. Naturally we are prone to entertain and nourish high presumptions of our own strength, and of our own wisdom.

a.) *Of our own strength.* In our prosperity we think ourselves able to carry any cross; we fancy ourselves strong enough to bear away even Samson's gates upon our shoulders, and prepared to encounter any affliction in the world. But when the hour of temptation comes, we find we are but like other men, and are ready to sink, with Peter, if but one wave rises higher than another. Usually sufferings, before they come, are like a mountain at a great distance, which seems so small that we think we could almost stride over it; but upon nearer approaches, when we come to the foot of it, it appears as if it would fall upon us, and crush us in pieces. Peter is so big with love to Christ, that he will die with him rather than forsake him; yea, though all the rest should betake themselves to their heels, he will stand by him to the last drop of blood; and yet behold, when it comes to the trial, a weak silly damsel is able with a single question to frighten him out of his confidence, and he doth not only forsake, but forswear his Lord. Pendleton, in the book of martyrs will fry out a fat body in flames of martyrdom, rather than betray his religion; but when the hour comes that Christ and religion had most need of him, he had not one drop of all that fat to spare for either.

b.) As we are prone to presume of our own strength, so we are very apt to idolize *our own wisdom*—to lean to our own understanding, and think by our policy to wriggle ourselves out of any labyrinth of trouble and perplexity. But we find it otherwise when we come into the snare, we then are forced to cry out with the Church, "He hath hedged me about that I cannot get out, he hath made my chain heavy" (Lamentations 3:7). Like a malefactor that has broken out of prison, he thinks to run away, but he has a heavy chain upon his heel that spoils his haste; and being fenced in round about, he goeth to this corner, hoping to find some gap, but there he finds the hedge made up with thorns; and to another corner, and there also the briars stop him. But that is not all; read on in the Church's complaint, and you shall find greater obstructions, "He hath enclosed my ways with hewn stones" (v.9). Suppose a man would venture the scratching of his flesh to break through a hedge to save his life, yet that would not do, God had taken away the hedge, and built a wall instead of it—a wall so high that they could not clamber over, a wall so thick that they could not dig through. The meaning is, man in affliction thinks to make his way through by his own art and cunning, but upon the attempt he finds difficulties arising still higher and higher, so that when all is done, escape is impossible without an immediate rescue by the arm of omnipotence.

This was Paul's case, "When we came to Asia, we were pressed out of measure beyond strength, insomuch that we despaired even of life" (2 Corinthians 1:8); a great strait, in all probability it was that uproar at Ephesus, wherein Paul was like to have been pulled in pieces, for it was a trouble that befell him in Asia (Acts 23:10); a strait wherein the apostle was at his wit's end; he despaired even of life, 'We were bereft of all counsel how to expedite ourselves out of the danger.'

So David complains, "How long shall I take counsel in my soul?" (Psalm 13:2). When he was persecuted by Saul, and beset with innumerable dangers, he took counsel; he thought of this means and the other means; cast about this way and that way how to escape, but in vain; all his counsels left him as full of sorrow and despair as they found him; "How long shall I take counsel in my soul, having sorrow in my heart?" He had his sorrow for his pains.

Thus it was with the apostle, all his counsel left him in the hand of despair, "We despaired even of life": his case was no other than the prisoner at the bar, at the time the sentence of death is passed upon him; he looks upon himself (and so do standers by) as a dead man; he is legally dead, dead to all intents and purposes of the law; there lacks nothing but the execution. So it was with Paul, "We had the sentence of death in ourselves" (2 Corinthians 1:9); the sentence was passed in his own breast, and now saith Paul, 'I am but a dead man.'

This was his strait, and it seemed God had a design in it, and what was that? He himself will tell you, "We had the sentence of death in ourselves, that we should not trust in ourselves, but in God which raiseth the dead."

See here that the design is expressed both negatively and affirmatively. *Negatively*, "that we might not trust in ourselves," for God saw even in that great apostle himself a disposition to self-confidence, a proneness to be exalted above measure, through the abundance of revelations; and therefore so as to prick the bladder of pride, God gave him a thorn in the flesh to work out this self-trust. God reduced him to a state of despair as to outward and visible probabilities. *Affirmatively*, "But in God which raiseth the dead": by this desperate exigence God would teach Paul ever after where strength and counsel were to be had in the like extremities; nowhere but in God and him abundantly. The God of resurrections can never be nonplussed; he that can raise the dead can conquer the greatest difficulty; he that can put life into dead men can put life into dead hopes and raise up our expectations out of the very grave of despair; that God can put life into dead bones, is a consideration able to put life into a dead faith.

To this purpose it is very observable that even those to whom God hath indulged the largest proportions of faith and courage, he hath allowed not only to languish under fears, but even to despair under insupportable difficulties before they could recover holy confidence in God. We find David, that great champion of Israel, more than once surprised with dreadful fear: "I said in my haste" (Psalm 31:22; 116:11). The Hebrew signifies (*in trepidatione mea*, or, *in festinatione mea*) 'in my trembling, in my precipitancy': or, as the Septuagint translates it, 'in my ecstacy,' when I was almost beside myself for fear. Well, what did he say then? Why he said, "I am cut off from before thine eyes" (Psalm 31:22); that is, 'God hath cast me out of his care, he looks no more after me, I am a lost man.' And again, "I said in my haste, 'All men are liars'" (Psalm 116:11)—'Even Samuel himself, that told me I should be a king, he hath seen but a false vision, and a lying divination; God never said so to him. No, I shall one day fall by the hand of Saul.'

And thus the prophet Jeremiah laments, "Thou drewest near in the day that I called upon thee; thou saidst, 'Fear not'" (Lamentations 3:57); but before God spake a 'fear not' to his soul, he was afraid to purpose; hear what he saith, "They have cut off my life in the dungeon, and cast a stone upon me; waters flowed over mine head, then I said, 'I am cut off'" (vv.52-54). Mark ye, with Paul, he had received the sentence of death in himself, he looks upon himself as a dead man, yea as already in his grave, and his gravestone laid upon it, "They have cut off my life in the dungeon, and cast a stone upon me," dead and buried, and a stone rolled to the mouth of the sepulchre.

And thus you may hear Jonah crying in the whale's belly, "I am cast out of thy sight" (Jonah 2:4). And Zion, in the dust, tuning her lamentations, "The Lord hath forsaken me, and my Lord hath forgotten me" (Isaiah 49:14). It were easy to multiply instances.

Now this is continually our case, and this is still God's design; we are proud creatures, full of self-confidence, and therefore God, by strange and unexpected providences, doth hedge up our way with thorns, and wall up our path with hewn stones, bringing to despair even of life, bereaving us of counsel, driving us from all our own shifts and policies, bringing us under the very sentence of death—all that we might not trust in ourselves but in God who raises the dead. He unbottoms us by despair, convinces us of our impotence and folly, shows us what babes and fools we are in ourselves, so that in all our future hazards and fears we might know nothing but God, "Go in the strength of the Lord, and make mention of his righteousness, and of his only" (Psalm 71:16). And thus you see Peter, who before was so confident that he thought all the world might forsake Christ sooner than himself, afterward he was convinced of his own infirmity and instability when Christ, to put him in mind of his three-fold denial, put him upon that three-fold interrogatory, "Simon Peter, lovest thou me more than these?" (John 21) in other words, 'than the rest of thy fellow disciples,' durst make no other answer but this, "Lord, thou knowest"; he pleads nothing but his sincerity; and for that also, he casts himself rather upon Christ's trial than his own; "Lord, thou knowest."

14. *By affliction God makes himself known unto his people.* How long do we hear of God before we know him? We get more by one practical discovery of God than by many sermons; "I have heard of thee often by the hearing of the ear, but now mine eye seeth thee, therefore I abhor myself in dust and ashes," crieth Job upon the dunghill (Job 42:5-6). In the Word we do but *hear* of God, in affliction we *see* him.

Prosperity is the nurse of atheism; the understanding being clouded with the streams and vapors of those lusts which are incident to a prosperous estate, men grow brutish, and the reverence and sense of God is by little and little defaced; but now by affliction the soul (being taken off from sense-pleasing objects) hath a greater disposition and liberty to retire into itself, and being freed from the attractive force of worldly allurements, the apprehensions are wont to be more serious and pregnant, and so more capable of divine illumination. The clearer the glass is, the more fully doth it receive in the beams of the sun. When the warm breath of the world hath blown upon us, we are not so capable of the visions of God.

The wicked, through the pride of his heart, will not know God; they say to the Almighty, "Depart from us, for we desire not the knowledge of thy ways" (Job 21:14). "Who is the Lord?" saith Pharaoh (Exodus 5:2). And truly the very godly themselves are exceeding dark and low in the apprehensions of God; our ignorance of God being never perfectly cured till we come to heaven, where we shall see him face to face, and know him as we are known (1 Corinthians 13:12). In the meantime, by the strokes of divine vengeance God makes the wicked know him to their cost; so by the rod of correction he makes his people to know him to their comfort. As God brought all his plagues upon Pharaoh's heart, that he might know who the Lord was in a way of wrath; so he lays affliction upon the loins of his people, that they may know him in a way of love; "Israel shall cry unto me, 'My God, we know thee'" (Hosea 8:2).

Moses never saw God so clearly as when he descended in a cloud. And truly that dispensation was but a type of the method which God uses in making himself known unto his saints; he puts them into the clefts of the rock, covers them with his hand while he passes by, and then proclaims his name before them, "The Lord, the Lord God, merciful and gracious" (Exodus 33:19-23). The people of God have the most sensible experience of his attributes in their sufferings; his holiness, justice, faithfulness, mercy, and all-sufficiency—

a.) *His holiness.* Affliction shows what a sin-hating God our God is; for though his chastisements on his Church are in love to their persons, they are in hatred to their corruptions. While he saves the sinner, he destroys the sin, "By this shall the iniquity of Jacob be purged, and this is all the fruit to take away his sin" (Isaiah 27:9). If the soul is to live, sin must die.

b.) *His justice.* Afflictions are correction to the godly and punishment to the wicked; in both God is righteous. Thus Israel knew God; "Howbeit thou art just in all that is come upon us, for thou hast done right, but we have done wickedly" (Nehemiah 9:33). In the severest dispensations they judge themselves and justify God; yea, when they cannot discern his meaning they adore his righteousness: "Righteous art thou, O Lord, when I plead with thee; yet let me talk with thee of thy judgments; wherefore doth the way of the wicked prosper?" (Jeremiah 12:1). When the soul is unsatisfied, yet God is not unjustified.

c.) *His faithfulness.* Faithfulness in the very affliction itself, "I know, Lord, that thy judgments are right, and that thou in faithfulness hast afflicted me" (Psalm 119:75). Faithfulness to his covenant; for affliction is not so much threatened as promised to believers; but of this hereafter. The more David was afflicted, the more God's faithfulness appeared. 'Oh,' says the holy man, 'I could not have wanted a stroke of all that discipline wherewith my heavenly Father hath chastised me.'

He is faithful in hearing the prayers of his suffering saints. This poor man cried and the Lord heard him, and saved him out of all his troubles. Even when David lacked faith, God lacked not faithfulness. "I said in my haste, 'I am cut off from before thine eyes'; nevertheless thou heardest the voice of my supplications when I cried unto thee" (Psalm 31:22).

Unbelief itself cannot make the faithfulness of God of no effect. I conceive these words of the apostle to bear this sense, "If we believe not, yet he abideth faithful, he cannot deny himself" (2 Timothy 2:13). It is not to be understood of a *state* of unbelief, but of an *act* of unbelief; not of a lack *of* faith, but a lack *in* faith; neither of which can render God unfaithful, who is engaged not so much to our faith, as to his own faithfulness to himself, to hear the prayer of his troubled servants; "Call upon me in the day of trouble, I will deliver thee, and thou shalt glorify me" (Psalm 50:15).

Believers experience this faithfulness of God best in their sufferings because—

[1.] *Then they are most prayerful.* When our elder brother Esau is upon us, we can wrestle with our elder brother Jesus, and not let him go until he bless us.

[2.] *Then they are most vigilant to observe the returns of prayer.* "My voice shalt thou hear in the morning, in the morning will I direct my prayer unto thee, and will look up" (Psalm 5:3). In adversity we are early with God in prayer; "In the morning shalt thou hear my voice, in the morning will I direct my prayer"; it implies double earliness, and double earnestness in prayer. And when we have done praying, we shall begin waiting, "I will look up." In prosperity we put up many a prayer that we never look after; God may deny or grant, and we hardly take notice of it. But in affliction we can press God for the returns of prayer; "Hear me speedily, O Lord, my spirit faileth, hide not thy face from me, lest I be like to them that go down into the pit" (Psalm 143:7); not only denials but delays kill us; then we can hearken for the echo of our voice from heaven, "I will hearken what God the Lord will say, for he will speak peace to his people" (Psalm 85:8). As God cannot easily deny the prayer of an afflicted soul, so if he grant, we can take notice of it, and know our prayers when we see them again; "This poor man cried, and the Lord heard him" (Psalm 34:6); and this endears the heart to God and to prayer. "I love the Lord, because he heard my voice and my supplications; because he hath inclined his ear unto me, therefore will I call upon him as long as I live" (Psalm 116:1-2).

As faithfulness in hearing prayer, so also in making good the promise: the afflicted soul can witness unto God, "as we have heard, so have we seen" (Psalm 48:8). What we have heard in the promise, we have seen in the accomplishment, God was never worse than his word. As affliction is a furnace to try the faith of God's people, so it is also to try the faithfulness of God in his promises; and upon the trial the Church brings in her experience, "The words of the Lord are pure words, as silver tried in a furnace of earth purified seven times" (Psalm 12:6). Let a man cast the promise a thousand times into the furnace, it will still come out full weight: "As for God, his way is perfect, the word of the Lord is tried" (Psalm 18:30). It is to be understood in both places of the word of the promise; a man may set heaven and earth upon a promise, and it will bear them up.

d.) *His mercy*—Mercy in the moderation of chastisements. In the midst of judgment he remembers mercy. "It is of the Lord's mercies that we are not consumed, because his compassions fail not" (Lamentations 3:22), cries the Church in Babylon. It is banishment, but it might have been destruction; we are in Babylon, but we might have been in hell; it of the Lord's mercies, and his mercies alone, that we are not there. So saith the afflicted soul: 'If my burning fever had been the burning lake, if my prison had been the bottomless pit, if my banishment from society with friends had been expulsion (with Cain) from the presence of God, and that forever, God would have been righteous in it.' It is never so bad with the people of God, but it might have been worse; anything on this side hell is pure mercy.

And as mercy in moderating, so mercy in supporting; "When I said my foot slippeth," now I sink, I shall never be able to stand under this affliction, I cannot bear it, "Thy mercy, O Lord, held me up" (Psalm 94:18). When David was sinking, God put under him his everlasting arms and held him up, as Christ stretched forth his hand to save Peter when he began to sink. Even when God's suffering people have not any great raptures, yet then they find sweet supports, "His left hand was under me, his right hand embraced me" (Song of Solomon 2:6).

And yet it is not supporting mercy only which they experience in their sufferings, but often his refreshing, his rejoicing mercy; so it follows in the psalm above cited, "In the multitude of my thoughts within me, thy comforts delight my soul" (Psalm 94:19). My thoughts were dark and doleful, and full of despair, and not a few of them; multitudes broke in upon me, and even swallowed me up; but thy comforts were light and life, and delight to my soul, my thoughts did not sink me so deep, but thy comforts raised me up as high; my thoughts were a hell, but thy comforts were a heaven within me.

The soul *hears* of God's mercy in prosperity, but it *tastes* of his mercy in affliction; and as it were overcome with enjoyments, can call to others, "O taste and see how good the Lord is" (Psalm 34:8). Hence it is, that of all the days of the year the apostle would choose as it were a Good-Friday, a passion day, to rejoice in; "God forbid I should rejoice in anything but in the cross of Jesus Christ" (Galatians 6:14); Christ's sufferings for him, and his sufferings for Christ.

e.) *The all-sufficiency of God* is the last attribute I mentioned, which God proclaims before his suffering people; "Now thou shall see," saith God to Moses, "what I will do to Pharaoh" (Exodus 6:1). Hitherto thou hast seen what Pharaoh hath done to Israel, now thou shalt see what I can do to Pharaoh; and so they did see the doubling of their burdens was the dissolving of their bondage; the extinguishing of their line was the multiplying of their seed; the same waters which were Israel's rocks were the Egyptians' grave. "I will pursue, I will overtake, I will divide the spoil; my lust shall be satisfied upon them; I will draw my sword, my hand shall destroy" (Exodus 15:9); so boasts the proud tyrant, 'I will, I will, I will'; but not so fast Pharaoh, let God speak the next word, "Thou didst blow with thy wind, the sea covered them, they sank as lead in the mighty waters" (Exodus 15:10). O sudden turn! There lieth Pharaoh with all his boastings, drowned in the sea. Thus did God appear to his oppressed Israel in the very nick of their extremities. In the thing wherein they dealt proudly, God was above them, and "Israel saw that great work which the Lord did upon the

Egyptians; and the people feared the Lord and his servant Moses" (Exodus 14:31).

"Israel saw"—in prosperity God works, but we see him not; affliction opens our eyes; when we see our dangers, then we can see God in our deliverances. God could have brought Israel into the Land of Promise by a shorter cut, in forty days: but he leads them about in a howling wilderness forty years (not a more likely place in all the world to have starved them and their flocks), and why? But to proclaim to Israel and all succeeding generations, "That man liveth not by bread alone, but by every word that proceedeth out of the mouth of the Lord, doth man live" (Deuteronomy 8:3). Israel learned more of God's all-sufficiency in a land of drought than she could have learned in the land flowing with milk and honey; namely, that God can feed without bread, and satisfy thirst without streams of water; that he can make the clouds rain food, and the rock give out rivers; that the creature can do nothing without God, but God can do what he please without the creature.

Instances are endless—In a word, suffering time is the time wherein God makes his attributes visible, "The Lord will be a refuge to his people, a refuge in time of trouble"; and what follows? "And they that know thy name will put their trust in thee" (Psalm 9:9-10). In the school of affliction God reads lectures upon his attributes, and expounds himself unto his people, so that many times they come to know more of God by half a year's sufferings, than by many years' sermons.

15. *God teaches them in a suffering condition to mind the duties of a suffering condition, to study duty more than deliverance, and seriously to enquire what it is which God calls for under the present dispensation.* The soul crieth out with Paul, when laid for dead at Christ's feet, "Lord, what wilt thou have me to do?" (Acts 9:6). There is no condition or trial in the world, but it gives a man opportunity for the exercise of some special grace, and the doing of some special duty; and that is the work of a Christian—in every new state, and in every new trial, to mind what new duty God expects, and what new grace he is to exert and exercise.

To mind deliverance only is self-love, which is natural to man, "The captive exile hasteneth that he may he loosed, and that he should not die in the pit" (Isaiah 51:14). Man in affliction would eagerly be delivered, have the burden taken off, and the yoke broken; he makes more haste to get his afflictions removed than sanctified. But this is not the work God looks for; no, nor to think only what a man would do if he were delivered. 'O,' thinks one, 'if God would heal me of this sickness, deliver me out of this distress, I would walk more closely with him; I would be more abundant in family duties; I would be more fruitful in my converse; I would do thus and thus,' and so on.

Now though men should sit down in their afflictions, consider their ways, and make new resolutions for better things if God shall give better times; yet if this is all, it may be nothing else but a wile of the deceitful heart, a temptation and snare of the devil, to gain time as it were of God; a mere diversion to turn aside the heart from the present duty which God expects. And therefore when God intends good and happiness to the soul by the present chastisement, he pitches the soul upon the present duty, which is to "hear the rod, and who hath appointed it" (Micah 6:9); to discern God's aim, and to find out the meaning of the present dispensation—to say to God, "I have born chastisement, I will not offend anymore; that which I see not teach thou me, and if I have done iniquity, I will do no more" (Job 34:31-32). To reflect upon our ways and spirits, to complain of sin, and not of punishment, "Wherefore doth a living man complain? A man for the punishment of his sin? Let us search and try our ways, and turn again to the Lord" (Lamentations 3:39-40). To think the present condition the best; "I have learned in whatever state I am, therewith to be content" (Philippians 4:11). In patience to possess our souls, to rejoice in God even in tribulation. To mind the public calamities of the Church more, and our private sufferings less; to pray for the welfare of Zion, "In thy good pleasure do good unto Zion" (Psalm 51:18). To live upon Jesus Christ, and to make him glorious by our afflictions, "That Christ may be magnified in our bodies, whether it be by life, or by death" (Philippians 1:20). Paul studied more how to adorn the cross than to avoid it;

how to render persecution amiable; and if he must suffer for Christ, yet that Christ might not suffer by him; that Christ might be exalted, and the Church edified. And lastly, to commit the keeping of our souls to God in well-doing, as unto a faithful Creator.

16. *In the school of affliction another lecture which the Holy Ghost reads is, 'The Fruits and Advantages of a Suffering Condition'.* There is in every state of life a snare and a privilege; and it is the folly and misery of man, left to himself, that he willingly runs into the former but misses the latter; he is only able to add to his own misery, and to make his condition worse than he finds it. Those whom God loveth he teacheth; he teacheth them to study, as the duty of their present state, so the advantage. When God takes away creature comforts, he doth not only necessitate, but by the secret impressions of love upon the heart, he emboldens the soul to look out for reparations, and to urge God for a recruit in some richer accommodations; "Lord," saith Abraham, "what wilt thou give me, seeing I go childless?" (Genesis 15:2). In like manner, 'Lord, what wilt thou give me,' saith a suffering saint, 'since I go wifeless, and friendless, and landless, and houseless,' and so forth. So the disciples, "Lord, we have forsaken all and followed thee, what shall we have therefore?" (Matthew 19:27). Faith may be a loser for Christ, but it will not be a loser by Christ; and accordingly Christ makes answer, "Verily I say unto you, there is no man that hath left house, or brethren, or sisters, or father, or mother, or children, or lands, for my sake, and the gospel's, but he shall receive an hundred fold now in this life" (Mark 10:29-30).

Advantage enough! A hundred for one was the best year that ever Isaac had: but how shall this be made good? Why with "persecution—houses, and brethren, and sisters, and mothers, and children, and lands, with persecution" (v.30): this must make up the account. It is very observable, that year wherein Isaac received his hundred fold was Isaac's suffering year; the year wherein famine had banished him from his own country to sojourn with Abimelech in Gerer; yet Isaac's best harvest was in a year of famine; and this was typical to all the children of promise: they must receive Isaac's increase, "a hundred fold with persecution."

And I conceive our Saviour may allude to this type in this promise. In persecution the people of God find their hundred fold; when they make a Scripture enquiry, they find sufferings, especially those for Christ's sake, to be their letters testimonial for heaven—the pledge of adoption—a purge for corruption—the improvement of holiness—and, the enhancement of glory. In a word, whatever the affliction is, that shall be the soul's gain, "All things work together for good to them that love God" (Romans 8:28). This God teaches his people; it is the very design of the eighth chapter to the Romans, and of the twelve first verses of the twelfth chapter to the Hebrews, to show that God's rod and God's love go both together. This quiets the heart, and supports the soul under its burden, "For this cause we faint not"; why? because "though our outward man perisheth, yet the inward man is renewed day by day" (2 Corinthians 4:16). As if he had said, 'What we lose in our bodies we gain in our souls; what we lose in our estates we get in grace'; thus they bear up and comfort themselves in their deepest sorrows, while they that lie poring upon their afflictions and are witty only to aggravate every circumstance of a suffering condition sink their own spirits, vex their souls, dishonour God by slandering his dispensations, and bring up an evil report upon the Cross of Jesus Christ. The spiritual privileges of God's suffering people are therefore called "the peaceable fruits of righteousness" (Hebrews 12:11) because the taste of this fruit brings such peace and comfort into the soul as makes it rejoice not in God only, but in tribulation; and in all these things to account itself "more than conqueror through him that hath loved us" (Romans 8:37).

17. *By his chastisements God teaches what Christ taught Martha, that is, the one thing needful; affliction discovers how much we are mistaken about our must-be's, our necessaries.* In our health and strength and liberty we think this and that thing must be done; we think riches, honors, and a good name in the world necessary; we must get estates and lay up large portions for our children; we must raise our families and call our lands after our own names, and the like.

But in the day of adversity, when death looks us in the face, when God causes the horror of the grave, the dread of the last judgment, and the terrors of eternity to pass before us, then we can "put our mouths in the dust, smite upon our thigh, and sigh with the breaking of our loins" (Lamentations 3:29; Jeremiah 31:19; Ezekiel 21:6), O how have I been mistaken? "How have I fed upon ashes, and a deceived heart turned me aside, so that I could not deliver my soul, nor say, 'Is there not a lie in my right hand?'" (Isaiah 44:20) Only then can we see that pardon of sin, interest in Christ, evidence of that interest, a sense of God's love, a life of grace, and an assurance of glory, are the only indispensibles. In a word, that Christ alone, is the *unum necessarium* (the one thing needful) and that all other things are but "loss and dung" in comparison of "the excellency of the knowledge of Christ Jesus the Lord, and of interest in him, and in his righteousness" (Philippians 3:8), without which the soul is undone to all eternity.

Oh that Christians would be wise, that they would not "spend their money for that which is not bread, nor their labour for that which satisfieth not" (Isaiah 55:2), but labour for faith which might realize and substantiate unseen and spiritual things, and give them a being unto the soul! Those that will not learn this lesson in the school of the Word, shall learn it in the school of affliction if they belong to God, and therefore set your heart to it.

18. *Time redemption is another lesson which God teaches to those whom he corrects.* In our tranquility, how many golden hours do we throw down the stream, which we are likely never to see again; for one whereof the time may come, when we would give rivers of oil, the wealth of both the Indies, mountains of precious stones (if they were our own), and yet neither would they be found a sufficient price for the redemption of any one lost moment. It was the complaint of the heathen moralist, and may be much more our complaint, "Who is there amongst us that knows how to value time, and prize a day at a due rate?" Most men study rather how to pass away their time, than to redeem it; and are prodigal of their precious hours, as if they had more than they could tell what to do withall: our season is short, and we make it

shorter. How sad a thing is it to hear men complain, 'O what shall we do to drive away the time?'

Alas, even sabbath-time, the purest, the most refined part of time—time consecrated by divine sanction—how cheap and common is it in most men's eyes, while many do sin away, and the most do idle away, those hallowed hours? Seneca was wont to jeer the Jews for their ill husbandry, in that they lost one day in seven, meaning their Sabbath. Truly it is too true of the most of Christians, they lose one day in seven, the Sabbath for the most part is but a lost day; while some spend it totally upon their lust, and the most (I had almost said the best), do fill up the void spaces and intervals of the Sabbath from public worship, with idleness and vanity! But oh when trouble comes, and danger comes, and death comes; when the sword is at the bowels, the pistol at the breast, the knife at the throat, death at the door, how precious would one of those despised hours be? Evil days cry with a loud voice in our ears, 'Redeem the time.' That caution was written from the tower in Rome, "Redeem the time, because the days are evil" (Ephesians 5:16). In life-threatening dangers, when God threatens as it were, that time shall be no more, then we can think of redeeming time for prayer, for reading, for meditation; for studying and clearing out our evidences for heaven; for doing and receiving good, according to opportunities presented; yea, then we can gather up the very broken fragments of time, that nothing may be lost. Then God teaches the soul what a choice piece of wisdom it is for Christians (if it were possible) to be before-hand with time; for usually it comes to pass through our unskillfulness and unwatchfulness, that we are surprised with death; and we that reckoned upon years, many years yet to come, have not possibly so many hours to make ready our accounts. It may be this night the summon may come, and then if our time be done, and our work to be begun, in what a case are we! The soul must needs be in perplexity at the hour of death, that sees the day spent, and its work yet to do. A traveller that sees the sun setting when he is but entering on his journey cannot but be aghast. The evening of our day, and the morning of our task, do not well agree together; the time which remains is too short to lament the loss of past time. By such hazards God doth come upon the soul as the angel upon Peter in prison, and smites upon our sides, bids us rise up quickly and gird up ourselves; and bind on our sandals, that we may redeem lost opportunities, and do much work in a little time. It is a pity to lose anything of that which is so precious and so short.

19. *Affliction teaches how to estimate, at least to make some remote and imperfect guess, at the sufferings of Jesus Christ.* In our prosperity we pass by the cross carelessly and regardlessly; at the best we do but shake our heads a little; the reading of the story or Christ's passion stirs us up some pity towards him, and passion against his persecutors; but it is quickly gone; we forget as soon as we get into the world again; but now let God pinch our flesh with some sore affliction; let him fill our bones with pain and set us on fire with a burning fever; let our feet be hurt in the stocks, and the irons enter into our souls; let our souls be exceedingly filled with the scorning of those that are at ease, and with the contempt of the proud; let us be destitute, afflicted, tormented, and so forth, then happily we shall sit down and look upon him whom we have pierced, and begin to say within ourselves, 'And are the chips of the cross so heavy? What then was the cross itself, which my Redeemer did bear? Are a few bodily pains so bitter? What then were those agonies which the Lord of glory sustained in his soul? Is the wrath of man so piercing? What was the wrath of God, which scorched his righteous soul, and forced his very heart's blood through his flesh in a cold winter's night, so that his sweat was as great drops of blood falling down to the ground? Are the buffetings of men so grievous? What were the buffetings of Satan, which our Lord sustained, when all the brood of the serpent lay nibbling at his heels? Is a burning fever so hot? How then did the flames even of hell itself scald my Saviour's spirit?' Christ felt *poenasin fernales*, though not *inferni*.

Is it such a heart-piercing affliction to be deserted of friends? What was it then for him, that was the Son of God's love, the darling of his bosom, to be deserted of his Father, which made him cry out to the astonishment of heaven and earth, "My God, my God, why hast thou forsaken me?" (Matthew 27:46). Is a chain so heavy, a prison so loathsome, the sentence and execution of death so dreadful? O what was it for him that made heaven and earth to be bound with a chain, hurried up and down from one unrighteous judge to another, mocked, abused, spit upon, buffeted, reviled, cast into prison, arraigned, condemned, and executed in a most shameful and accursed manner? O what was it for him to endure all this contradiction of sinners, rage of the devil, and wrath of God, in comparison of whom the most righteous person that ever was, may say with the penitent thief on the cross, "And we indeed justly, but he, what evil hath he done? He made his grave with the wicked, and with the rich in his death, because he had done no violence, neither was any deceit in his mouth" (Luke 23:41; Isaiah 53:9). Blessed be God, my prison is not Tophet, my burnings are not unquenchable flames, my cup is not filled with wrath; in a word, this is not hell. Blessed be God for Jesus Christ, by whom I am delivered from wrath to come. And thus, as the Lord Jesus by the sensible experience of his own passion, came perfectly to understand what his poor members suffer while they are in the body, so we by the remainders of his cross, which he hath bequeathed us as a legacy, come in some measure to understand the sufferings of Christ, or at least by comparing things of such vast disproportion, to guess at what we cannot understand.

20. *The last lesson which God teaches by affliction is how to prize and long for heaven.* In our prosperity, when the candle of God shines in our tabernacles, "when we wash our steps in butter, and the rock poureth us out rivers of oil" (Job 29:6), we could set down with the present world, and even say with the disciple (though not upon so good an account), "It is good for us to be here; let us here build us tabernacles" (Matthew 17:4); while life is sweet, death is bitter; and heaven itself is no temptation, while the world gives us her friendly entertainments. But when poverty and imprisonment, reproach and persecution, sickness and sore diseases, do not only pinch but vex our hearts with variety of aggravations; we are not so fond of the creature, but we can be content to entertain a parley with death, and take heaven into our consideration. Not that merely to desire to be in heaven, because we are weary of the world, is an argument

of grace, or a lesson that needs divine teaching; self-love will prompt as much as that comes to. But because like foolish travellers, we love our way though it be troublesome, rather than our country; God by this discipline taketh off our hearts by degrees from this present world, and makes us look homeward, being burdened we groan, and with the dove, we return to the ark when the world is afloat round about us. When David was driven from his palace, then "Woe is me that my pilgrimage is prolonged" (Psalm 120:5-6); so the Septuagint renders it. We should be contented like the Israelites with the garlic and flesh-pots of Egypt, if God did not set cruel taskmasters over us to double our burdens; and when God hath thus lessened our esteem of the world, he discovers to us the excellency of heavenly comforts, and draws out the desires of the soul to a full fruition; "When shall I come and appear in thy presence?" (Psalm 42:2). "Even so, come Lord Jesus" (Revelation 22:20). Afflictions make heaven appear as heaven indeed. To the weary, it is rest; to the banished, home; to the scorned and reproached, glory; to the captive, liberty; to the soldier, conquest; and to the conqueror, it is a crown of life of righteousness and of glory. To the hungry, it is hidden manna; to the thirsty, the fountain of life; to the grieved, fullness of joy; and to the mourner, pleasures forevermore. In a word, to them that have lain upon the dunghill, and kept their integrity, it is a throne on which they shall sit and reign with Christ for ever and ever.

Surely beloved, heaven thus proportioned to every state of the afflicted soul, cannot but be very precious, and will make the soul with a stronger or weaker impulse, desire to be dissolved and to be with Christ, which is best of all. A Christian indeed is comforted by faith, but not satisfied; or if satisfied, it is in point of security, not of desire; because here we are absent from the Lord, and walk by faith, not by sight. Hope, though it keeps life in the soul, yet it is not able to fill it; he longs, and thinks every day a year till he be at home. They that walk by faith, cannot be quiet till they are in the sight of those things which they believe. Jacob, when he heard that Joseph was alive, though he did believe it, yet could not be satisfied with hearing of it; but saith he, "I will go and see him before I die" (Genesis 45:28): so the believing soul, 'He, whom my soul loveth, was dead, but is alive, and behold he liveth forevermore. I will die that I may go and see him,' as Augustine, upon that answer of God to Moses, "Thou canst not see my face and live" (Exodus 33:20), makes this quick and sweet reply, "Then Lord let me die that I may see thy face."

Thus have I presented you with those twenty several lessons which Jesus Christ, the great Prophet of his Church, teaches his afflicted ones in the school of affliction.

CHAPTER TWO

The Nature or Properties of Divine Teaching

I now come to the second thing; namely, the nature or properties of divine teaching.

For my brethren, it is not every teaching that wilt make or evidence a man to be a blessed man under affliction. There is hardly any man that is under affliction but he learns somewhat by it, and yet few are blessed. The reason is, because it matters not so much what a man is taught, as who is the teacher, whether he be taught of God or no. Yea, that is not all either, for we are not to enquire only *whether* we are taught of God, but *how*; there is a twofold teaching of God. There is a common teaching which even the heathen, men out of the Church, hypocrites, and reprobates within the Church, may have; there is a special teaching, proper and peculiar only to the children of promise. A covenant teaching; "All thy children shall be taught of God" (Isaiah 54:13); it is the covenant of God with the Redeemer. A teaching without which there is no profit, "I am the Lord thy God, which teacheth thee to profit," so to profit by chastisements and corrections: so it followed, "which leadeth thee by the way that thou shouldest go" (Isaiah 48:17). God's teachings are not only directing teachings, but leading teachings; not only to show the way, but to enable to go in the way.

Now this teaching hath six properties.

1. *It is an inward teaching.*

a.) Inward in respect of *the object.* So our Saviour, concerning the saving teaching of the Holy Ghost, "When the Spirit of truth is come, he will guide you into all truth" (John 16:13). Man may lead you *unto* truth, but it is the Spirit of God only that can lead you *into* truth; he only that hath the "key of David, that openeth and no man shutteth, and shutteth and no man openeth" (Isaiah 22:22), can open to you the door of truth, and show you the inside of truth. And great is the difference between these two teachings. He that comes to a stately house or palace, sees only the outward fabric and structure; and even that may take much; but he that comes into it, sees all the inward contrivances and conveniences; he sees all the rich furniture and adornings of the several rooms and offices of the house which are not only for use, but for delight and ornament; surely the very outside of truth is goodly; but, like the king's daughter, "it is all glorious within" (Psalm 45:13); not pleasing only, but ravishing. Those who are led into truth see this, by virtue whereof David saw wonderful things in the law, objects which filled his soul with wonder and delight (Psalm 119:18). And as the teachings of the covenant are inward in respect of the object, so also—

b.) Inward in respect of *the subject*; "In the hidden part thou hast made me to know wisdom" (Psalm 51:6). And again, "I thank the Lord who gave me counsel, my heart also instructs me in the night seasons" (Psalm 16:7). The heart is the most inward part of the body, and the night season the most retired and private time; both express the intimacy of divine teaching. "God, who commanded light to shine out of darkness, hath shined into our hearts, to give the light of the knowledge of the glory of God in the face of Jesus Christ" (2 Corinthians 4:6); it is a full expression, and holds forth the inward teachings of God, both in reference to the subject, and to the object.

[1.] In reference to *the subject,* he that "commanded the light to shine out of darkness, hath shined into our hearts"; man's light may shine into the head, but God's light doth shine into the heart. God hath his throne in heaven; but his chair—his pulpit—is in the heart; he hath "shined into our hearts."

[2.] And then you have the inwardness of divine teaching in respect of *the object;* he hath given us "the light of the knowledge of the glory of God in the face of Jesus Christ." Man may give knowledge, confused general knowledge, but God gives the light of knowledge in the lustre and brightness of it. "In thy light we shall see light" (Psalm 36:9); the soul sees by the same light whereby God himself sees thy light; and not only so, here is not only knowledge and light of knowledge, but the glory of that light—the light which God brings into the sanctified understanding is a glorious light, a marvelous light; the soul that the Spirit of God taketh by the hand and leads into truth stands wondering at the glory and excellency of that light which shines round about it.

And then lastly, all this "in the face of Jesus Christ"; the face is the full discovery of a person. Moses could not see God's face, but only his back parts he might see. But now by the flesh of Jesus Christ, God hath put a veil upon his face; the veil of his flesh, through which we may see the face of God; for now in Christ it is God manifest in the flesh, the human nature of Jesus Christ hath made God visible. In this face now of Jesus Christ do they whom God teaches by a saving gospel teaching see divine truth; they see it now — not only by borrowed representations and natural resemblances, but in its own native beauty and lustre — as the truth is in Jesus.

2. *Divine teaching is a clear, convincing teaching.* So our Saviour said of the Spirit, "When he is come, he shall convince the world" (John 16:8); the word signifies a clear demonstrative conviction. So the apostle defines faith to be the evidence, or demonstration, the evident demonstration of things not seen (Hebrews 11:1). The Holy Ghost, in his teachings, brings in divine truths with such a clear and convincing light, that the soul sits under it fully satisfied; it is not only convinced to silence, but to assurance; the soul doth freely acquiesce in the present truths; "Now I know," saith Moses' father-in-law, "that the Lord is greater than all gods" (Exodus 18:11). He had heard that before, but now he is thoroughly convinced. So David concerning his afflictions, "I know, Lord, that thy judgments are right, and that of faithfulness thou hast afflicted me" (Psalm 119:75). He was fully satisfied both of the equity and fidelity of God's chastisements; right in respect of the merit, and faithful in respect of the end. And thus in all the lessons before presented to your view, and in all other, what God teaches, he teaches with such a clear evidence of truth, that the soul is set beyond all peradventure: "Our gospel came unto you, not in word only, but in power and in the Holy Ghost, and in much full assurance" (1 Thessalonians 1:5): the word hath a double and a triple emphasis, assurance, full assurance, and much full assurance; such are the teachings of the Holy Ghost.

Common teaching may so convince, that a man cannot tell how to gainsay or contradict, but the understanding may remain doubtful still. There is not a full and clear assent in the understanding to the truths propounded; but a man remains, in the apostle's language, "a double-minded man" (James 1:8); or as the word signifies, 'a double-souled man' (*duplex animo*), a man of a double or divided spirit, floating between different opinions; one soul (as it were) believeth this way, and another soul believeth that way; one, while he believeth there is a God, and shortly thereafter the fool saith in his heart, "There is no God" (Psalm 14:1); sometimes he calls sin evil; and then again he thinks it good. He believeth, and he believeth not; sometimes what he hears from the Word is the truth of God, sometimes he thinks again it is but an invention of man. But now the teachings of God set a man beyond all those fluctuations and unsettledness in judgment. There is that which the apostle calls "the riches of the full assurance of understanding to the acknowledgment of the mystery of God" (Colossians 2:2); assurance of principles, even when the soul may possibly lack the assurance of application.

3. *Divine teaching is experimental teaching.* The soul can speak experimentally of the truths it knows; "It is good for me," saith David, "that I have been afflicted" (Psalm 119:71); why, but may not any man say as much as that? Yes, few men there are but have the notion in their heads and in their lips; but mark, the psalmist speaks experimentally to the point, and doth instance the good which he had gained by affliction, "I have learned thy statutes." He had learned more acquaintance with, delight in, and conformity to the Word—he knew it more, and loved it better, and was more transformed into the nature of it than ever. So again, "The Lord preserveth the simple" (Psalm 116:6), in other words, God stands by his upright-hearted ones to secure them from violence; a good notion, but any man may have it in the proposition. But David hath it in the experience, "I was brought low and he helped me"; my faith, my comfort, and my resolutions were brought low, "my feet had well-nigh slipped" (Psalm 73:2); but God helped my faith, revived my comfort, strengthened my resolutions, and established my

feet. Thus St. Paul, "I know whom I have believed" (2 Timothy 1:12); I have experienced his faithfulness and his all-sufficiency; I dare trust my all with him. "I am sure he will keep it safe to that day."

And thus they that are taught of God in affliction can speak experimentally, in one degree or another, of the gains and privileges of a suffering condition. They can speak experimentally of communion with God, "Though I walk through the valley of the shadow of death, I will fear no evil" (Psalm 23:4). Why? "For thou art with me": I have had comfortable experience of thy upholding, counseling, comforting presence with me in my deepest desertions; so of other fruits of affliction, this I have got by my sufferings; I bless God, I have learned more patience, humility and self-denial; to be more sensible of my brethren's sufferings; to sit looser to the world, to mind duty, and to trust safety with God; to prepare for death, and to provide for eternity.

Common knowledge rests in generals, and lies more in propositions than in application; but they that are taught of God can say, "As we have heard, so have we seen" (Psalm 48:8); they can go along with every truth, and say, 'It is so, I have experienced this word upon mine own heart,' they can set to their seal that God is true.

4. *Divine teaching is a powerful teaching.* After a man hath got many truths into the understanding, the main work is yet to do, and that is to bring down holy truths to action, to draw forth divine principles into practice. A natural man may know much, he may have a heap of truths in his understanding; but they all lie strengthless in the brain; he hath no power to live the truths he knows. Covenant teachings convey strength as well as light, and do what they teach. "The Lord spake to me with a strong hand, and instructed me that I should not walk in the way of this people, saying, 'Say ye not a confederacy.' neither fear ye their fear, nor be afraid" (Isaiah 8:11-12). It is a most sweet and comfortable Scripture, both in respect of what it implies and what it expresses. First, it implies this much, that even the holy prophet himself had no small combat and conflict within himself, what to do in such a juncture of time as that was, when it was told the house of David, saying, "Syria is confederate with Ephraim"

(Isaiah 7:2): that is, that both those kingdoms had made a league together, and were now upon their march with their combined forces, to make war against the house of David. It was sad news, and the text saith, "The heart of Ahaz, and the heart of the people was moved, as the trees of the wood are moved with the wind"; they were terribly afraid, even ready to die for fear, and in that fear abundance of the people fell off to the enemy, and engaged with them; as it is intimated, "They refuse the waters of Shiloh that go softly" (Isaiah 8:6). They looked upon the forces of Jerusalem as poor and inconsiderable, and in no way able to oppose and engage so potent an adversary as came against them; and so deserted their own party, and rejoiced in Rezin and Remaliah's son. To cover their defection from their true sovereign, they cried up the invaders as their best friends, who came to rescue them from the tyranny and oppression of Ahaz. And it seems the prophet Isaiah himself was surprised with fear too, for a time, and began to dispute the matter within himself, whether it were not best for him to strike in with the stronger side, and to engage in the confederacy with two princes as the multitude did; there wanting not probably, fair and specious pretences to justify that defection. It seems, I say, that the prophet had a sore temptation upon his spirit about this matter, and was even ready to determine the question in the affirmative, till God came in and instructed him; and that is the second thing, the comfort expressed in these words. While the prophet was thus conflicting and fluctuating in his own thoughts, God came in, and by strength of hand rebuked his fears, silenced his objections, quieted his spirit, determined the dispute, and instructed him what course to take, which was not to comply, but to believe; to study duty, and leave safety with God, "Fear not their fear, nor be afraid, sanctify the Lord of Hosts himself." Power went forth with instruction, taught him what to do, and enabled him to do what it taught. Blessed be God, who has a hand to teach his people with, as well as a mouth; a hand of power, as well as a mouth of instruction: had it not been for this, the prophet himself would have been carried down the torrent of apostasy as well as others.

There is caution in this instance as well as comfort, in reference to ourselves, and our brethren; and that is, in case of surprise by some sudden gusts of fear and temptation, not rashly to judge ourselves or our brethren, but wisely and calmly to consider, "It is no other temptation than what is common to man" (1 Corinthians 10:13), yea to the best of men: Job, and David, and Jeremiah, and Habakkuk, and Peter, and here Isaiah, were all nonplussed, and staggered for a time, and recovered only by a powerful word from heaven; and therefore in such cases, it becomes Christians to pity rather than to insult; and to study to heal, rather than to reject, "considering themselves lest they also be tempted" (Galatians 6:1). This is the privilege of the children of promise, strength goeth out from the covenant with instruction, the Lord "who commandeth light to shine out of darkness, hath shined into our hearts" (2 Corinthians 4:6). God hath taught us by such a word, as that whereby he made the world, a creating word, a word that giveth strength as well as counsel. And it is this teaching which the prophet David so frequently importuneth in his prayers, "Teach me, O Lord, the way of thy statutes, make me to go in the paths of thy commandments; teach me to do thy will" (Psalm 119:33-36). Mark that, not only teach me *the way*, but teach me *to go*; not only teach me *thy will*, but teach me *to do thy will*. Common teaching may teach the way, but only saving teaching teaches *to go in that way*: an unregenerate man may know the will of God, but he knoweth not how to do that will.

5. *The teachings of God are sweet and pleasant teachings.* "Thou hast taught me"; what follows? "How sweet are thy words unto my taste! Sweeter than honey unto my mouth" (Psalm 119:102-103): he rolled the Word and promises as sugar under his tongue, and sucked from thence more sweetness than Sampson did from the honey-comb. Luther said he would not live in paradise, if he must live without the Word; but with the Word, saith he, "I could live in hell itself." There cannot but be much spiritual joy in divine teaching, because the Spirit doth accompany the truths, and so irradiate them with his own beauty and glory, that they do not only affect but ravish the heart, "Thy word is pure, therefore

thy servant loveth it" (Psalm 119:140). The prophet saw a beam of divine excellency sitting upon the Word, and that did happily engage his soul. Truth is burdensome to unsound spirits, because convincing; and they labour to extinguish that light which disturbs their quiet, "They hold the truth in unrighteousness" (Romans 1:18); they imprison the truth, and will not suffer it to do its office; but saving teaching is sweet and delightful, because it is suitable to the renewed part; to which it comes in with fresh comforts, to relieve and fortify it against the assaults of opposite corruption. I say, it is always sweet in that respect; but never more sweet than in affliction; the bitterness of adversity giving a more delicate relish unto the Word, by healing the distempers of the spiritual palate: and then the soul cries out with Jeremiah in the prison, "Thy words were found, and I did eat them, and thy Word was unto me the joy and rejoicing of my heart" (Jeremiah 15:16).

6. *And lastly, divine teaching is an abiding teaching.* "The anointing which ye have received of him abideth in you" (1 John 2:27). Mere notional knowledge is transitory and inconsistent, leaving the soul dubious and uncertain. Observe how the apostle James expresses it, speaking of the mere notional hearer, "He beholdeth himself, and goeth his way, and straitway forgetteth what manner of man he was" (James 1:24). Observe, he doth not only forget what he heard, but he forgets what he *was*: the glass, whether the Word or affliction, discovered to him his spots, showed him his pride, his covetousness, the impurity of heart and life, and so forth, but he went away and forgot what manner of man he was; he forgets the Word, he forgets the rod, and what both rod and Word discovered to him, together with the resolutions and promises made to God in both. A godly man may forget the Word (a gracious heart may have a bad memory) but he will not so easily forget himself; he doth not forget his spots, and that keeps him in continual work, to wash and purge himself from all filthiness of flesh and spirit, "Remembering mine affliction and my misery, the wormwood and the gall: my soul hath them still in remembrance, and is humbled in me" (Lamentations 3:19-20).

"Teach me, O Lord," says David, "the way of thy statutes, and I will keep it unto the end" (Psalm 119:33). He dares promise perseverance, if God will undertake instruction; and accordingly he made good his promise, upon this very account, "I have not departed from thy judgment, for thou hast taught me" (Psalm 119:102), observe it—he doth not say, 'I *will* keep thy statutes'; but he can say, and that many years after, "I *have* kept thy statutes."

Many will say in their affliction, 'I will keep thy statutes'; promise fair, if God will but deliver them; but how few can say with David, "I have kept"—I have not departed from—"thy judgments"! "Of old time," saith God, "I have broken thy yoke, and burst thy bonds, and thou saidst, 'I will not transgress'; when upon every high hill, and under every green tree thou wanderest, playing the harlot" (Jeremiah 2:20). Good words in trouble, but poor performance out of trouble; no sooner out of affliction, but they fall again to their old course of spiritual adultery against God; no sooner their old hearts and their old temptations meet, but they close, and embrace one another; "They started aside like a broken bow" (Psalm 78:57). But David was taught of God, and therefore he is as careful to make good his vows, as to make good vows; "I will pay thee my vows, which my lips have uttered, and my mouth hath spoken, when I was in trouble" (Psalm 66:13-14). The after-part of David's life was much more severe and exact then the former: "I have not departed from thy judgments, for thou hast taught me" (Psalm 119:102).

These are the properties of divine teachings; but lest I should lay a snare before the blind, and make the heart sad which God would not have made sad, I must of necessity lay in a few brief cautions.

1. This must not be understood as if God taught all at first—either all truth, or all of any one truth. God does not teach all his lessons at the first entrance into the school of affliction (at least not usually—for we dare not limit him). The fruits of affliction are not gathered presently, "No chastening for the present seemeth joyous, but grievous; nevertheless *afterwards* it yieldeth the peaceable fruits of righteousness unto them which are exercised thereby" (Hebrews

12:11). Teaching is the fruit of affliction, it must have a rip-
ening time; and therefore, O thou discouraged soul, say not
God doth not teach thee at all, if he does not teach thee all at
once. "The entrance of thy word giveth light" (Psalm
119:130); God lets in light by degrees; usually he teaches his
children, as we teach ours, now a little, and then a little;
somewhat this week, and more next week; somewhat by this
affliction, and more by the next affliction. It is not to be despised if God discovers to the soul the need of divine teaching,
and engages the heart in holy desires and longings after it; so
that the afflicted soul can say in sincerity, "My soul breaketh
for the longing that it hath unto thy judgments at all times"
(Psalm 119:20).

2. It is not to be understood as if he taught all alike. God
hath several forms in the school of affliction, as well as in the
school of the Word; there are fathers for experience, young
men for strength, and babes for the truth and being of grace.
And therefore if God has not taught thee so much as another, say not he hath not taught thee at all. "As one star differs
from another in glory" (1 Corinthians 15:41), so also is the
school of Christ. It is free grace thou art a star, though thou
art not a star of the first or second magnitude; that God hath
let in some divine light, though not so much light as another
may possibly have; that thou art in God's school, though it
may not be in the highest form. In point of holy emulation,
we should look at the degrees of grace; but in point of thankfulness and comfort, we should look at the truth and being
of grace.

3. When we say that God teaches powerfully and abidingly, it is not to be understood as if these teachings did put the
soul into an immutable evenness of spirit, or free it from all
insurrections and disturbances from opposite corruption.
Such a frame of soul is only the privilege of the glorified
state, wherein we shall see God face to face, and dwell in
immutability itself to all eternity. Here the Church (like the
moon) hath its fulls and its wanes. David had his sinkings,
and Job his impatient fits. We "have heard of the patience of
Job" (James 5:11), yea, and of his impatience too. Moved,
the taught of God may be, but not removed; fall they may,
but not fall away; fearfully, but not finally; terribly, but not

totally. But these things are inseparable with covenant teaching.

a.) The soul is thereby made sensible of the least stirrings and whisperings of corruption. "I find a law in my members warring against the law of my mind" (Romans 7:23): others have it, but they do not find it; they are not sensible of the law in their members, and so forth.

b.) They are exceedingly displeased with the opposition they find in their natures against the teachings of God, and do rise up in indignation against all that contradiction which is in the unregenerate part, in any kind whatever; "Why art thou cast down, O my soul? And why art thou so disquiet within me?" (Psalm 43:5). Is there cause for this despondency? Is this done like a David? Like "a man after God's own heart" (Acts 13:22)? Is this the fruit of all the experiences of God's faithfulness and all-sufficiency? And so in other cases doth the soul chide down distempers and improper workings of spirit; the soul is full of displeasure against itself; "So foolish was I, and ignorant, as a beast before thee" (Psalm 73:22); it cannot find words bad enough to give itself.

c.) And if that will not do, then they go to God in prayer, and spread their temptations before the Lord, "O my God, my soul is cast down within me" (Psalm 42:6). When they cannot lay the storm, and still the tempest by their own word, then, with the disciples in the ship, they go to Christ, and desire him by his powerful word to rebuke it, that there may be a calm; they go and pray out their distempers, and pray their hearts in a better frame; as once it was said of Luther, that when he found distempers upon his spirit, he would never give over praying till he had prayed his heart into that frame he prayed for.

d.) By virtue of the teachings of God, they are enabled to maintain opposition against all that opposition which they find in their own spirits; "As the flesh lusteth against the spirit, so the spirit lusteth against the flesh" (Galatians 5:17). The spiritual regenerate part doth as naturally rise up and make war against the flesh, and fleshly motions, as the flesh doth against the teachings of God in the spiritual part. Opposition is not maintained only by precept and rules, but naturally, and by virtue of an inward antipathy; the spirit lusteth; the spiritual opposition is as suitable and agreeable to the new nature, as the sinful opposition is to the old nature. Hence is the life of a believer called a wrestling, a warfare (Ephesians 6:12).

e.) Not only so, but by the help of divine teaching the soul gets ground of that fleshly opposition wherewith it is molested, by degrees. "In the day when I cried, thou answeredst me; and strengthenedst me with strength in my soul" (Psalm 138:3). Prayer brought in God, and God brought in strength, whereby he got ground of his distempers; and though all was not done at first, yet his comfort was, all should be done in God's time. "The Lord will perfect that which concerneth me" (Psalm 138:8); I am not perfect, but I shall be perfected; "He that hath begun a good work, will perform it till the day of Jesus Christ" (Philippians 1:6).

f.) Though the soul is not always the same for temper and acting, yet it is always the same for purpose and design; "Then shall I not be ashamed, when I have respect unto all thy commandments" (Psalm 119:6). Though he could not keep all, he could respect all the commandments of God. "My soul presseth hard after God" (Psalm 63:8); crowds of opposition intercepted and disturbed his sweet and constant communion with God sometimes; but he broke through that crowd by main strength to recover God's presence again, "My soul presseth hard after thee," and Paul is pressing after perfection when he could not overtake it.

g.) And lastly, the soul hath not always, possibly, the same relish and taste of divine truths and ordinances, but it hath the same estimate; it keeps up high thoughts of spiritual things, and when it cannot relish them, yet even then it doth hunger after them, "My soul breaketh for the longings it hath unto thy judgments at all times" (Psalm 119:20).

And yet even in reference to these dispositions, which I call inseparable concomitants to saving teachings, I must add this one caution in close of all, namely, *that allowance be made in case of desertion.*

A child of God, for causes which here we cannot stand to mention, may be cast into so deep a state of desertion for a time, that he may (as the apostle speaks) "forget that he was purged from his old sins" (2 Peter 1:9). A child of light may walk in darkness. And though there be no such decay in the new man, wherein both habits and acts do cease, yet they may be so stupefied by the impressions of the present temptations, as the poor soul shall be sensible of neither, but reduced as it were into such a state as when grace was but an embryo in the womb; that spiritual life shall be almost extinguished; there may be life, but no sense of that life.

More might be added, but I am sensible how this discourse swells beyond the proportion I intended, and therefore must hasten. Thus much, therefore, for the second thing propounded in the doctrinal part, the nature and properties of divine teaching.

CHAPTER THREE

How Affliction Lieth in Order to Instruction

I come now to the third thing propounded, namely, to enquire how affliction lieth in order to instruction? What tendency chastisement hath to promote the teachings of God in the soul? What use God makes of correction to this end?

It is true, there is need of an arm of omnipotence to make chastisement to have a saving influence upon the heart; and so there doth also even in the Word itself; and divine ordinances—they do not save by an intrinsical virtue, or power of their own, but there is a passive fitness in them to serve omnipotence for divine and saving ends; a fitness of instrumentality, as there is in a saw to cut, and in a wedge to cleave, and so forth. The instrument can do nothing alone, but there is a fitness in it to serve the hand of the workman.

Thus it is, in a proportion, with affliction. It is true, there is not so immediate and direct a tendency in the rod, as there is in the Word, to teach and instruct the children of God; yet there is in chastisement a subserviency to prepare the heart of man, and to put it into a better disposition to comply with divine teaching, than naturally it is capable of. Christ works in the hot furnace; the most excellent vessels of honour are formed there: Manasseh, Paul, and the jailer were all chosen in this fire; as God saith, "I have chosen thee in the furnace of affliction" (Isaiah 48:10). Grace works in a powerful, yet in a moral way. God speaks when we are most apt to hear, congruously yet forcibly, by a fit accommodation of circumstances, which you may discover in these four particulars:

1. *By correction God takes down the pride of man's heart.* There is not a greater obstruction to saving knowledge than pride and self-opinion, whereby man either thinks he knows enough, or that what God teaches is not worth learning. Therefore it is proclaimed before the word, "Hear and give ear, be not proud, for the Lord hath spoken" (Jeremiah 13:15). In divine matters, as well as human, "only by pride cometh contention" (Proverbs 13:10). It is pride which raises

objections against the Word, and disputes the commands, when it should obey them.

The proud men in Jeremiah, when they could elude the message of God by his prophet no longer, did at length stiffen into downright rebellion. First, they shift, "Thou speakest falsely" (Jeremiah 43:2); and then they resolve, "As for the word thou hast spoken to us in the name of the Lord, we will not hearken unto thee"; be it Baruch, or be it God, we will have none of it: "But we will certainly do whatsoever goeth forth of our own mouth" (Jeremiah 44:16-17). Such a masterpiece of obduration is the heart of man, that it stands like a mountain before the Word, and cannot be moved till God comes with his instruments of affliction, and digging down those mountains, casts them into a level, and then God may stand, as it were, upon even ground, and talk with man. This pride of heart speaks loud in the wicked, and whispers too audibly even in the godly; it is a folly bound up even in the hearts of God's children, till the rod of correction drives it out; and then the poor bleeding wretch cries, "Lord, what wilt thou have me to do?" (Acts 9:6).

2. *Affliction is God's forge, wherein he softens the iron heart.* There is no dealing with the iron while it remains in its own native coldness and hardness. But put it into the fire, make it red hot there, and you may stamp upon it any figure or impression you please. "God maketh my heart soft" (Job 23:16), saith Job; melted vessels are impressive to any form. So it is with the heart of man; naturally it is colder and harder than the northern iron, and that native hardness is much increased by prosperity, and the patience of God towards sinners; the iron sinew will rather break than bend. It is only the hot furnace that can make it pliable and impressive to God's counsels; therefore God resolves on this course, "I will melt them and try them" (Jeremiah 9:7); and sometimes God is forced to make the furnace seven times hotter, to work out that dross which renders men so uncomfortable to the ministry of the Word, while "God sends his prophets, rising up early, and sending them; and yet they will not incline their ear, but harden their necks against divine instruction" (Jeremiah 25:4, 17:23).

When the earthly heart of a man is so dried and hardened by a long sunshine of prosperity that the plough of the spiritual husbandman cannot enter, God softens it with showers of adversity, making it capable of the immortal seed, and blesses the springing thereof. The seed falls upon stony ground till God turn the stone into a heart of flesh.

3. *By chastisement man is made more attentive unto God.* In prosperity the world makes such a noise in a man's ears that God cannot be heard, "He speaks indeed once and twice," again and again, very often, "yet man perceiveth it not" (Job 33:14); he is so busy in the crowd of worldly affairs, that God is not heeded.

In the godly themselves there is much unsettledness and giddiness of mind. Our thoughts are naturally vain and scattered, the spirit slippery and inconsistent; which is a great impediment to our clear and full comprehensions of spiritual things, and therefore God deals with man as a father with his child playing in the marketplace, and will not hear or mind his father's call. He comes and takes him out of the noise of the tumult, carries him home, lays him upon his knee with the rod in his hand, and then the father can be heard. So doth God, I say, with his children, "He openeth their ears" (Job 36:10) which the world had stopped, and then instruction will enter.

When Joab would not come to Absalom, he sets his field on fire; and thus after neglects, God brings us to treat with him by affliction. God saith, as it were, "Come, let us reason together" (Isaiah 1:18); and the soul echoes back again, "Speak, Lord, for thy servant heareth" (1 Samuel 3:10): and when the soul is thus silent unto God, he comes and seals instruction by his Spirit.

4. And lastly, *affliction is an eye-salve, whereby God opens the eye of the soul to see the need and excellency of divine teaching, by the discovery of its own brutish ignorance of God, and of his ways, under all divine administrations;* as Ephraim once bemoaned himself to the Lord, "I have been as a bullock unaccustomed to the yoke" (Jeremiah 31:18). The prophet David will interpret it, "So foolish was I, and ignorant, and like a beast before thee" (Psalm 73:22). By means of this discovery God draws out the heart into humble and

holy supplication for divine teaching; "That which I see not, teach thou me; and if I have done iniquity, I will do no more" (Job 34:32).

When or how cometh the sinner thus to put in for instruction? "Why," says he, "I have borne chastisement" (v.31a). Correction discovered the need of instruction, "That which I see not teach thou me" (v.32a); and thus Ephraim, "Thou hast chastised me, and I was chastised" (Jeremiah 31:18a); but blows alone will not do it; therefore it follows, "Turn thou me and I shall be turned" (v.18b). Though chastisement alone could not turn Ephraim, yet it made him see an absolute necessity of divine power to his conversion.

And when God hath brought the heart once into this frame, to see and be affected with the sense of, its own ignorance and impotency, and to lie in the dust at God's feet, humbly importuning an effectual teaching from heaven; if God should withhold it, he would fail of not his promise only, but his own counsel and designs; in reference to which "God cannot lie" (Titus 1:2); but when he hath prepared the heart to pray, he will cause his ear to hear. When God hath engaged the heart in holy desires of saving instruction, it is not mercy only in God, but faithfulness, to satisfy the desire of his own creation, "Good and upright is the Lord, and therefore he will teach sinners in the way" (Psalm 25:8).

Thus much for the third particular thing propounded for the opening of the doctrine; I come now to the fourth and last.

CHAPTER FOUR

The Grounds and Demonstrations of the Point

It must needs be a blessed thing when correction and instruction meet, if we consider,

1. *The lessons themselves which God teaches his people;* which are, as above shown: sympathy, moderation, self-denial, humility, self-knowledge, prayer, the Scriptures, evidences for heaven, evil of sin, communion with God, exercise of grace, life of faith, self-diffidence, knowledge of God, duties of suffering, privilege of suffering, the one thing necessary, time redemption, the sufferings of Christ, and the value of heaven.

Behold Christians! To be taught of God when chastised by him, is a blessedness compounded of twenty several precious ingredients.

2. *The nature and properties of divine teaching;* which is inwardly, clearly, experimentally, powerfully, sweetly, and abidingly.

This must needs be a blessed teaching; it being a teaching which possesses the soul of the excellencies which it discovers. Doctrinal and notional knowledge is a blessing, "Blessed," saith Christ to his hearers, "are your eyes, for they see, and your ears, for they hear" (Matthew 13:16): but to be taught these lessons with these qualifications; to be taught into the nature and image of the truth; to be taught into the possession of divine excellencies—this is blessedness indeed; blessedness in being; full, perfect, fruitful blessedness.

3. *A teaching chastisement is the fruit of God's distinguishing love.* Chastisements, simply considered in themselves, lie in common to all the sons and daughters of Adam since the fall. They are the fruit of that first apostasy, as well as of actual and personal departures from God.

Yea and deliverance also lieth in common. Providence dispenses deliverance to the worst of men. The 106th psalm is a psalm of promises made to the Church; but the next psalm is a psalm of providential dispensations to the world; and there, as you find affliction, so you may find deliverance also out of those afflictions, to be the portion of wicked men. Rebels, fools, and seamen—for the most part, not the most religious order in the world—all these are delivered out of their troubles. The worst of men, I say, share in this fruit of God's providential goodness, deliverance; but a teaching sanctified affliction is the privy seal of special love, "My loving kindness will I not take from him" (Psalm 89:33); "whom the Lord loveth he chasteneth" (Proverbs 3:12); that is to say, with a teaching chastisement. When Word and rod meet together, when correction and instruction kiss each other, they are the fruit of paternal affection, and therefore must needs have a blessing bound up in them.

4. *A teaching correction is a branch of the covenant of grace, which God hath made in Christ for the children of promise;* "All thy children shall be taught of God. They shall all know me from the least of them to the greatest" (Hebrews 8:11). By virtue of divine teaching, affliction is adopted a branch in the covenant of grace. The 89th psalm is a song of the new covenant, "I will sing of the mercies of the Lord" (v.1)—what mercies? Not providenced mercies only, but promise mercies, covenant-mercies; "I have made a covenant with my chosen" (v.3). And amongst the rest of the branches of the covenant, you shall find the rod and the whip have their place. "If his children forsake my law, and walk not in my judgments, then will I visit their transgression with the rod, and their iniquity with stripes" (vv.30-32). Behold rod and stripes standing here, not upon Mount Ebal, the mount of curses, as branches of a covenant of works, but upon Mount Gerizim, the mount of blessings, as branches of the covenant of grace. Affliction is not so much threatened as promised to Christ's seed: "My covenant will I not break" (v.34). When God seems even to break the bones and hearts of his people by sore and heavy strokes of correction, yet he does not break his covenant, "My covenant will I not break"; it is in order to the covenant when God chastiseth his children, and instructs them by his chastisements. Affliction separated from instruction, is pure wrath; but by a matrimonial covenant those two Scriptures, "I will visit—I will teach", are married together, and made one spirit, as in my text, and then they are pure grace. The covenant is the

Magna Carta of heaven, and contains a list of whatever the Father hath purposed, the Son hath purchased, and the Holy Ghost doth apply to the heirs of promise. The breasts of the covenant run nothing but the milk of spiritual blessings to the children of God.

5. *A teaching affliction is the purchase of Christ's death and bloodshed.* Christ died not to exempt his redeemed from suffering, but to sanctify their sufferings with his own blood; "I pray not that thou shouldest take them out of the world, but that thou shouldest keep them from the evil" (John 17:15): whatsoever Christ purchased, he prayed for; and this was one main privilege, not freedom from the evil of affliction, but from the evil of sin; "Sanctify them through thy truth; thy word is truth" (v.17): Christ's blood purchased nothing for us but blessings.

6. And lastly, *a teaching affliction is the result of all the offices of Jesus Christ.* As a king he chastens, as a prophet he teaches, and as a priest he hath purchased this grace of his Father, that the rod might blossom, that correction might be consecrated for instruction unto the redeemed. Behold, a sanctified affliction is a cup whereinto Jesus Christ hath wrung and pressed the juice and virtue of all his mediatory offices; surely that must be a cup of generous and royal wine, like that in the supper, a cup of blessing to the people of God.

And thus I have finished the fourth particular, propounded for the clearing and confirming of the doctrine, namely, the grounds and demonstrations of the point; and with it the whole doctrinal part of this great and blessed truth, namely, that it is a blessed thing when correction and instruction, Word and rod, go together.

CHAPTER FIVE

Use of Information

I come now to the use, for the improvement of the point. And it may serve for information and exhortation.

1. *If only those who are blessed whom God chastens and teaches, then affliction alone is not enough to evidence a man to be a happy man.* No man is therefore blessed because he is chastened; blows alone are not enough, either to evince or to affect a state of blessedness. "Thou hast chastised me, and I was chastised" (Jeremiah 31:18), cried repenting Ephraim; as if he had said, 'I have had blows enough, if blows would have done me good; nay, but under all the strokes and smitings of thy displeasure, I have been as a bullock unaccustomed to the yoke, unreachable and untractable; thou hast drawn one way, and I have drawn another; thou hast pulled forward, and I have pulled backward; all thy chastisements have left me as they found me, brutish and rebellious.'

Surely blows only may break the neck sooner than the heart. They are in themselves the fruit of divine wrath, a branch of the curse, and therefore cannot possibly of themselves make the least argument of God's love to the soul. Bastards have blows as well as children, and fools because of their transgression are afflicted.

And yet it is very sad to consider that this is the best evidence that the most of men have for heaven; because they suffer in this world, they think they shall be freed from sufferings in the world to come; and because they have a hell here, they hope they shall escape hell hereafter, they hope they shall not have two hells. Yes, poor, deluded soul, thou mayest and must have two hells without better evidence for heaven. Cain, and Judas, and millions of reprobate men and women, have two hells—one in this life, in torments of body, and horror of conscience; and another in the life to come, in unquenchable fire. And so must thou, unless thou get better evidence for heaven than the present misery which is upon thee. Thou mayest have a prison on earth, and a dungeon in hell; thou mayest now want a crumb of bread, and hereafter a drop of water; thou mayest now be the reproach of men, and hereafter the scorn of men and angels, and of God himself. Therefore "be wise to salvation, by working it out with fear and trembling, and giving all diligence, make your calling and election sure" (2 Timothy 3:15; Philippians 2:12; 2 Peter 1:10). God forbid that a man should take that for his security from hell, which may be but the foretaste of it: the pledge and aggravation of endless misery.

Objection. But doth not the Scripture say, "Whom the Lord loveth he chasteneth, and scourgeth every son whom he receiveth" (Hebrews 12:6)? And again, "As many as I love, I rebuke and chasten" (Revelation 3:19)?

Answer. Yes, but mark, I beseech you; though the Scripture saith, "Whom the Lord loveth he chasteneth," it doth not say, 'Whomsoever the Lord chasteneth he loveth.' Though it saith, "He scourgeth every son whom he receiveth," it doth not say, 'Whomsoever he scourgeth he receiveth as a son.' Christ saith, "As many as I love, I rebuke and chasten"; but he saith not, 'As many as I rebuke and chasten, I love.' These Scriptures include children, but they do not exclude bastards. They tie chastening to sonship, but not sonship to chastening. The sons are chastened, but all the chastened are not, therefore, sons. The beloved are rebuked, but all that are rebuked are not, consequently, beloved.

But that place in Job seems to say as much, "Behold, happy is the man whom God correcteth" (Job 5:17).

It is true; but one Scripture must interpret another. David must expound Eliphaz: "Happy is the man whom God correcteth," when instruction goeth along with correction, when chastisement and teaching accompany one another: "Blessed is the man whom thou chastenest, O Lord, and teachest him out of thy law" (Psalm 94:12). The Scripture doth not usually give things their names, but when they are made up of all their integrals; "Whoso findeth a wife, findeth a good thing, and obtaineth favour of the Lord" (Proverbs 18:22), in other words, a wife made up of Scripture qualifications; otherwise a man may, and many men do, find a plague in a wife, and have her from the Lord in wrath, and not in love.

Indeed chastening and affliction is an opportunity of mercy, a may-be to happiness, but not (singly) an evidence of happiness; lay no more upon it than it will bear; it is an opportunity, improve it; it is no more, do not trust it.

2. This doctrine informs us, that as affliction simply considered is not enough to make or evidence a man to be happy, so neither is it sufficient to conclude a man to be miserable; *no man is therefore miserable, because afflicted*. It may prove a teaching affliction, and then he is happy; and yet this is another mistake among men; and that both in reference to others, and to ourselves.

a.) In reference to *others*. People are very prone to judge them wretched whom they see afflicted. It was the miserable mistake of Job's friends to conclude him miserable because smitten; cursed, because chastened.

b.) In reference to *ourselves*. It is a merciless mistake, sometimes even of God's own children, to sit down under affliction, especially if sore and of long continuance; and conclude God doth not love them because he doth correct them. It seems to be the very case of the believing Hebrews; they judged themselves out of God's favour, because under God's frowns; not at all beloved, because so greatly afflicted and persecuted. And therefore it is that upon which the apostle, after he presented them with a large catalogue and list of the primitive martyrs before Christ, in the eleventh chapter, bestows the first part of the next chapter, to prove by reasons drawn from nature, and instances taken out of Scripture (the first whereof is that unparalleled instance of Jesus Christ); that God's love and God's rod may stand together.

The truth is, my brethren, there is nothing that can make a man miserable but sin; it is sin that poisons our afflictions. "The sting of death is sin" (1 Corinthians 15:56), and so we may say of all other evils, which militate under death as soldiers under their general—the sting of sickness is sin; and the sting of poverty is sin; and the sting of imprisonment and banishment is sin—so of every affliction. Take the sting out (which is done by the blood of Christ, and evidenced by divine teaching), "and they cannot hurt nor destroy in all God's holy mountain" (Isaiah 11:9). And therefore let no children of God be rash, to conclude hard things against themselves, and to make evidences of wrath where God hath made none. Let Christians on both sides look further than

the affliction itself; the Holy Ghost having long since determined this controversy by a peremptory decision, "No man
knoweth either love or hatred by all that is before them"
(Ecclesiastes 9:1). In other words, no man can make a judgment, either of God's love or hatred towards him, by any of
these outward dispensations. "He causeth his sun to shine
upon the evil, and upon the good; and sendeth rain on the
just, and on the unjust" (Matthew 5:45). The sun of prosperity shineth upon the dunghill as well as upon the bed of spic-
es; and the rain of adversity falleth upon the fruitful garden
as well as upon the barren wilderness; he judgeth truly of his
estate, that judgeth by the Word, and not by providence. Evidences of grace consist not in outward dispensations.

3. *Deliverance out of trouble is not enough to evidence or
make a man happy.* It is not said, 'Blessed is the man whom
thou chastenest, O Lord, *and deliverest him out of trouble*';
but, "Blessed is the man whom thou chastenest *and teachest*"
(Psalm 94:12). A man may get rid of the affliction, and yet
miss of the blessing. All the bread which men may eat without the sweat of their brows, is not therefore hallowed;
abundance may flow in without labour, and yet not without
a curse. A woman may be delivered from the pain of child-
bearing, and yet lie under the curse of child-bearing; an easy
travail is not an infallible symptom of a state of reconcilia-
tion; if there is not faith in Christ—who hath borne and
borne away the curse—a speedy and easy deliverance is no
more than God gives to the brute creatures; for "by him the
hinds do calve, and the wild asses bring forth their young"
(Job 39:1). A miscarrying womb may be a mercy, when a
mature and easy birth may be in judgment. A man may leave
his chains and his blessing behind him in prison; and the fire
of a fever may be extinguished, when the fire of hell is preparing for the sinner.

It is good to be thankful for—but extremely dangerous to
be contented with—a bare deliverance. I shall conclude this
branch with this note, which alone might have stood for a
distinct observation, that those prayers in troubles are not
best heard which are answered with a deliverance; but those
prayers are best heard which are answered with instruction.
Even of our blessed Saviour it is said, "In the days of his

flesh he offered up prayers and supplications, with strong crying and tears, unto him that was able to save him from death, and was heard, in that he feared" (Hebrews 5:7). How was he heard? Not in that, "Save me from this hour," but in that, "Father glorify thy name" (John 12:27-28); not in deliverance, but in instruction; for, for that he giveth thanks, "I will bless the Lord who hath given me counsel; my reins also instruct me in the night season" (Psalm 16:7). His Father taught him and strengthened him in his passion, and this was the hearing of his supplications. That is the best return of prayers which works our good—not our wills—and when God doth not answer in the letter, if he answer in the better, we are no losers by our prayers, and therefore when we have prayed, let us refer it unto God to determine the answer.

4. Hence we may learn *how to judge of our afflictions*, and of our deliverances from them. For you need not, as the Scripture speaks in another case, say "Who shall ascend up into heaven" (Romans 10:6), to look into God's book of life and death? Or, "Who shall descend into the deep" (v.7), the deep of God's secret counsels, to make report hereof unto us? But what saith the Scripture? "The word is nigh thee" (v.8a); the word of resolution to this enquiry, it is nigh thee, "even in thy mouth and in thy heart" (v.8b). That is to say, if thou canst evidence this to thine own soul, that instruction hath accompanied correction, that God hath taught thee as well as chastened thee, then thou art a blessed man, and thou shalt be saved; thou hast the word of him who is the author of blessedness, and is blessedness itself; "Blessed is the man whom the Lord chasteneth, and teacheth him out of his law" (Psalm 94:12).

And therefore peruse, I beseech you, that model of divine instructions or lessons, presented to you in the doctrinal part of this discourse; and then consider the properties of divine covenant teaching, and compare your hearts and those lessons together; and if the Spirit of God can bear witness to thy spirit, that thou art thus taught, happy art thou; bless the Lord, for the Lord hath blessed thee.

But now on the other side, when there is no interpreter to accompany affliction, to expound unto man the meaning of the Almighty in his chastisements, when there is not a divine sentence in the lips of correction, when the rod is dumb, or the creature deaf, and cannot hear the rod, and who hath appointed it, it is much to be feared, the stroke is not the stroke of God's children. O my brethren, it is sad when men come out of affliction the same as they went in; and yet it is much sadder, when it may be said of a man, as once it was said of Ahaz, "In the time of his distress he did trespass yet more against the Lord" (2 Chronicles 28:22). It was an aggravation of wickedness, concerning which we may say (as our Saviour of the alabaster box poured on his head), wherever the Scripture shall be preached in the world, there shall also this which this man did be published, "This is that King Ahaz" (v.22b). Surely it is a standing and a dreadful monument of reproach and infamy unto him unto all generations.

Christians, it is sad and dangerous beyond all expression, when affliction serves but as a gage to give vent to the pride and murmur, the atheism and enmity which is in men's spirits against the Lord, when afflictions are but as oil unto the fire to irritate corruption, and make it blaze more fiercely. To continue in habitual sins—against such proclamations to desist—is professed rebellion against God. The prophet brought a heavy indictment against Jerusalem when he said, "Thou hast stricken them, but they have not grieved; thou hast consumed them, but they have refused to receive correction. They have made their faces harder than a rock, they have refused to return" (Jeremiah 5:3). In such cases it is to be feared, the cup of affliction is a vial of wrath, and that the plagues of this life are but some previous drops of that storm of fire and brimstone, wherein impenitent sinners shall be scorched and tormented forever.

That Scripture speaks dreadfully to this purpose in Jeremiah, "They are all grievous revolters" (Jeremiah 6:28). The prophet Isaiah expounds it, "Ye revolt more and more" (Isaiah 1:5). Walking with slanders, they do not only revolt, but slander those that reprove their revolting; "They hate him that reproveth in the gate" (Amos 5:10).

They slander the prophets and their words. Nay, God himself doth not escape the lash of their tongues. They say,

"The way of the Lord is not equal" (Ezekiel 18:25). When they should condemn their own ways, they censure God's.

"They are brass and iron" (Jeremiah 6:28); they would pass for silver and gold, a sincere and holy people, while they are a degenerate and hypocritical generation. "They are all corrupters" (v.28b); they have deeply corrupted themselves. "They have corrupted all their doings" (Zephaniah 3:7); "They have corrupted the covenant of Levi" (Malachi 2:8), in other words, the worship, the ordinances, the truths of God. "The bellows are burnt in the fire" (Jeremiah 6:29), i.e. the lungs of the prophets, which have preached unto them in the name of the Lord, rising up early, and lifting up their voices like trumpets, "to tell Israel their transgressions, and the house of Jacob their sins" (Isaiah 58:1); and stretching forth their hands unto them all the day long, they are spent. "The lead is consumed" (Jeremiah 6:29), i.e. all the melting judgments and chastisements, which (as lead is cast into the furnace to make it the hotter) God added to the ministry of the prophets, to make the Word more operative, will do no good.

All this while, "The founder melteth in vain" (v.29), whether God the master-founder, or the prophets, God's founders, they all melt in vain. All their labour is lost; neither Word, nor rod, neither judgments nor ordinances, can stir them. They refuse to receive correction, they will not be taught. "The wicked are not plucked away" (v.29); they are the same that ever they were; the swearer is a swearer still, and the drunkard is a drunkard still, and the unclean person is unclean still, "The vile person will speak villainy, and his heart will work iniquity, to practice hypocrisy, and to utter error against the Lord" (Isaiah 32:6). The unjust are unjust still, and the ignorant are ignorant still; nothing will better them, wicked they are, and wicked they will be.

What follows? A formidable sentence; "Reprobate silver shall men call them" (Jeremiah 6:30). They would be counted silver, but it is reprobate silver, refuse silver, dross rather than pure metal: and their hypocrisy shall be made known to all men; "Reprobate silver shall men call them"; and happy they, if it were but the censure of mistaking men only; nay, but the searcher of hearts hath no better thoughts of them:

men do but call them so, because God called them so first; "Reprobate silver shall men call them, because the Lord hath rejected them." God hath cast them out as the founder casts out his dross to the dunghill, and they shall never stand among the vessels of honour, in whom the Lord will be glorified. A fearful sentence! The sum whereof is this, that when teaching goeth not along with correction, when men come out of the furnace, and lose nothing of their dross, it is a sad indication of a reprobate spirit, without timely and serious reflection, nigh unto cursing. "O consider this, you that forget God and his chastisements, lest he tear you in pieces, and there be none to deliver!" (Psalm 50:22).

5. We may learn that *they may be blessed whom the world accounts miserable.* The men of the world are incompetent judges of the estate and condition of God's children. The godly man's happiness or misery is not to be judged by the world's sense and feeling, but by his own; it lieth inward, save only so far as by the fruits it is discernible, and the world's faculty of judging is only outward, made up of sense and reason. "Therefore," said the apostle, "the spiritual man judgeth all things, yet he himself is judged of no man" (1 Corinthians 2:15); that is, he is able to judge of the condition of the men of the world, but the men of the world are not able to judge of his condition, because it is above their faculty. The natural man thinks the spiritual man under affliction to be miserable, but the spiritual man knows the natural man, in the midst of his greatest abundance and bravery, to be miserable indeed. Therefore may the saints in their trouble think it, with St. Paul, "a very small thing to be judged of man's judgment" (1 Corinthians 4:3). This is but man's day of judging; so the word signifies. God's day is coming, when things and persons shall be valued at another rate. Christ in his day shall not judge "after the sight of the eyes" (Isaiah 11:3), i.e. not as things appear to sense and reason; "nor after the hearing of the ears" (v.3b), i.e. according to the report of the world—"but with righteousness shall he judge" (v.4), he shall judge of things and persons as they are, and not as they appear.

In the meantime, this is also another comfort, "We have the mind of Christ" (1 Corinthians 2:16), the judgment of

Christ, by virtue whereof we are enabled, in our measure, to judge of things and persons, as Christ himself judges.

6. Is chastisement a blessing when accompanied with instruction? See then and admire the wisdom, power and goodness of God, who can make his people better by their sufferings! Who knows how to extract gold out of clay; to draw the richest wine out of gall and wormwood; that can turn the greatest evil of the body to the greatest good of the soul; the curse itself into a blessing; that can make the withered rod of affliction to bud, yea to "bring forth the peaceful fruits of righteousness to them that are exercised thereby" (Hebrews 12:11). Behold, I show you a mystery! Sin brought affliction *into* the world, and God makes affliction carry sin *out* of the world. Persecution is but the pruning of Christ's vine; the almond tree is said to be made fruitful by driving nails into it, letting out a noxious gum that hinders its fruitfulness. God never intends more good to his children than when he seems to deal most severely with them. The very heathen hath observed to us, "God doth not love his children with a weak effeminate affection, but with a strong masculine love, and had rather they suffer hardship than perish" (Seneca). "Whom the Lord loveth he chasteneth, and scourgeth every son whom he receiveth" (Hebrews 12:6). God will rather fetch blood, than lose a soul; break Ephraim's bones, than suffer him to go on in the frowardness of his heart; destroy the flesh, that the spirit may be saved in the day of the Lord Jesus. "We are chastened of the Lord, that we should not be condemned with the world" (1 Corinthians 11:32). His discipline is made up of severity and love; he doth chastise, but he will teach also, that his children may inherit the blessing: the discipline is sharp, but the end is sweet. "Bless the Lord, O my soul, and all that is within me bless his holy name. Bless the Lord, O my soul, and forget not all his benefits" (Psalm 103:1-2).

7. It shows us that *a suffering condition is not so formidable a thing as flesh and blood doth represent it.* It is ignorance and unbelief which slander the dispensations of God, and cast reproach upon the cross of Christ. He that heard the words of God, could by way of holy triumph ask this question, "Why should I fear in the days of evil?" (Psalm 49:5) as

if he had said, 'What is there in an afflicted estate so much to be dreaded? Let any man show me a reason, and I will give way to fear and despondency.'

O that the children of God in affliction, or entering upon sufferings, would sit down and dwell upon this consideration: the fruit and advantage which God knows how to bring out of all their sorrows. This would keep them from uncomely despondencies, and dejections of spirit; "For this cause we faint not," saith the apostle—for what cause? "While we look not at the things which are seen, but at the things which are not seen" (2 Corinthians 4:16,18); that is to say, not at the *visible* sufferings, but at the *invisible* fruit and advantage of our sufferings. This holds up the head and keeps up the heart, and makes the soul not only to be patient, but to "glory in tribulation; knowing that tribulation worketh patience, and patience experience, and experience hope; and hope maketh not ashamed, because the love of God is shed abroad in our hearts by the Holy Ghost which dwelleth in us" (Romans 5:3-5). This is the way to counterpoise the temptation; and in the conflict between the flesh and the spirit, to come in to the succour of the better part.

8. *It shows us the reason why God keeps some of his people so long under the discipline of the rod.* Truly God not only brings his children into the school of affliction, but many times keeps them long there. History and experience will afford instances without number. Hence you have the people of God so often at their 'How-longs' in their sufferings: "How long wilt thou forget me, O Lord, forever? How long wilt thou hide thy face from me? How long shall I take counsel in my soul? How long shall mine enemy be exalted over me?" (Psalm 13:1-2). In this psalm where my text is, "How long shall the wicked, how long shall the wicked triumph?" (Psalm 94:3). Twice "how long," before he can vent his complaint; and yet again the third time, "How long shall they utter and speak hard things?" (Psalm 94:4). "How long," cries Jeremiah, "shall I see the standard, and hear the sound of the trumpet?" (Jeremiah 4:21). And Zechariah, "O Lord of Hosts, how long wilt thou not have mercy on Jerusalem, and on the cities of Judah?" (Zechariah 1:12). The souls under the altar cry with a loud voice, "How long, O Lord,

holy and true, dost thou not avenge our blood on them that dwell on earth?" (Revelation 6:10).

Verily, God doth keep his people sometimes so long under their pressures, that they begin at length even to give themselves up to despair, and to conclude they shall never see deliverance. Thus you find not only the common multitude of the Jews in the Babylonian captivity, concluding desperately, "Our bones are dried, our hope is lost, we are cut off for our parts" (Ezekiel 37:11). Dry bones may as well live, as our captivity have an end; but even the prophet Jeremiah himself, "They have cut off my life in the dungeon, and cast a stone upon me" (Lamentations 3:53); he seems to himself to be in the condition of a man that is dead and buried, and the grave stone rolled to the mouth of the sepulchre; a metaphor expressing a hopeless and desperate condition.

Yea, hence it is that when deliverance is near, they cannot believe it, though a prophet of God, or an angel from heaven should report it: "Thou shall arise and have mercy upon Zion; for the time to favour her, yea the set time is come" (Psalm 102:13), sings someone that lived near the expiration of the seventy years' captivity; and yet in the meantime the Jews reply as before, "Our bones are dried, our hope is lost, we are cut off for our parts": as much as to say, 'Tell not us of God's arising; we shall never see Zion again, we are but dead men.' Observe it by the way, they that would not believe the captivity while it was in the threatening, would not believe deliverance when it was in the promise; a just judgment upon them, that they that would not believe God threatening, should not believe God promising. But that is not all, deliverance was so incredible after so long a captivity, that they could not believe it when they saw it; "When the Lord turned again the captivity of Zion, we are like them that dream" (Psalm 126:1). They knew not (as it fared with Peter), whether it was true, or whether they saw a vision only; 'Is this a real deliverance, or are we in a dream only?' Our Saviour tells us, that "When the Son of Man shall come," with particular deliverances to his Church, "he shall not find faith on the earth" (Luke 18:8); there will not be faith enough in the people to believe it, by reason of the long pressure and persecutions that have been upon them.

Now, what is the reason that God permits affliction to lie so long upon the backs of his children? Truly one is, because they have lived so long in sin; they have been long a-sinning, and therefore God is long a-correcting. God puts them to their "how longs," because they have put God to his "how longs." "How long refuse ye to keep my commandments, and my laws?" (Exodus 16:28). "How long will this people provoke me? And how long will it be ere they believe?" (Numbers 14:11). "How long shall thy vain thoughts lodge within thee?" (Jeremiah 4:14). "How long will it be ere they attain to innocency?" (Hosea 8:5). And truly if they have made God complain of their "how longs," no wonder if God makes them complain of his.

But then again, another and the main reason is, *because the work is not yet done*; they do not receive instruction by their correction, else affliction would quickly cease. God giveth not a blow, he draws not a drop of blood, more than is necessary, "For a season if needs be, ye are in heaviness" (1 Peter 1:6). If there is heaviness, there is need of it; and if heaviness continues long, there is need of it. It is not to gratify their enemies, that God keeps them so long under their lash, but to teach them; not that God afflicts willingly (Lamentations 3:33), but that he may "do them good in their latter end" (Deuteronomy 8:16).

Then they shall wait no longer for their deliverance. God will open the prison doors, and throw the rod into the fire. It is infinite mercy that they are not delivered till they are bettered; that God will not cease chastening till they are willing to cease sinning, saying, "I have borne afflictions, I will offend no more" (Job 34:31).

9. Notice from this *what unteachable creatures we are by nature*, who will not set our hearts to receive instruction till we be whipped to it by the rod of correction, and hardly then neither. Unless God multiply stripes, it is not multiplying of precepts that will do us good; there must be stripe upon stripe, and affliction upon affliction, as well as "line upon line, and precept upon precept" (Isaiah 28:10), or else it is in vain. We should say, that we were a very bad child, that will be taught no longer than the rod is upon his back! Such are we; we are so unteachable that we put God, as it were, to

study what methods and courses to take with us. "How shall I do for the daughter of my people? I will melt them and try them" (Jeremiah 9:7).

10. And lastly, it shows us on the contrary, *how much gracious hearts are in love with the Word*, for the improvement of their spiritual knowledge, when they can put such an estimate upon their sufferings, and account that their blessing which other men call their misery; "Blessed is the man whom thou chastenest and teachest" (Psalm 94:12). The psalmist in another place speaks warmly to this purpose; "It is good for me that I have been afflicted," why? "That I might learn thy statutes" (Psalm 119:71). He loves the Word so dearly, that for the Word's sake, he is in love with affliction. The whip, the rod, the prison, the wilderness, anything is precious that brings instruction with it. Carnal people can be content to die in their ignorance, so that they may die in their nest; whereas gracious hearts think not much to go to school to a bridewell; and even while the blood is running down the back, can say it is good, because they are taught by it. O the different account that grace and nature make of the same dispensation! It is proud disdain to scorn to be taught by the lowest of God's ushers; the treasure is precious though in an earthen vessel (2 Corinthians 4:7). There are none too old, none too wise, none too high, to be put into the meanest school on this side heaven.

CHAPTER SIX

Use of Exhortation

I have done with the use of information, I come now in the second place to the use of exhortation, *firstly*, to such as are yet free from sufferings, *secondly*, to such as are under sufferings, and *finally*, to such as are come out of a suffering condition.

1. The first branch of exhortation is *to such as through the patience and forbearance of God are yet free from chastisement and affliction.* The candle of the Almighty doth shine in their tabernacle, and "wash their steps in butter" (Job 29:6). Now, would ye prevent chastisement, and keep off the strokes of divine displeasure from yourselves or families? Let me commend unto you, a two-fold caution from this doctrine.

a.) *If you would prevent chastisements, study these and the like lessons well, while ye are under the teachings of the Word.* Therefore doth God send us into the school of affliction, because we have been non-proficients in the school of the gospel; because we will not hear the Word, God turns us over to a severer discipline, and to have our ears bored with affliction; and then saith God, 'Now hear the rod, and who hath appointed it.' O my beloved, labour I beseech you, to profit much by the teachings of Jesus Christ in the gospel; set your hearts to all truths and counsels of God revealed to you therein. The gospel is the model or platform of sound words, able to make you sound Christians, wise to salvation; O let your profiting be made known unto all men. In special, set you hearts to those instructions or lessons first propounded; for the neglect whereof God sends his people into captivity, that there he may teach them with the briars and thorns of the wilderness, in particular.

Learn in the time of your peace and tranquility to lay to heart the sufferings of the rest of your brethren that are in the world. Remember them that are in bonds, as bound with them; put your souls in their souls' steads; and content not yourselves with those loose, fruitless, and transient glances which those that are at ease in Zion do usually cast upon men in misery; a cold 'Lord have mercy upon them,' and there's an end. Remember them that are in bonds, as bound with them; and that you may know you are not to confine your compassion to prisoners only, it follows, and them that suffer adversity. Learn to sympathize with all the people of God under any adversity whatsoever; hide not your eyes, and shut not up your bowels of compassion from any that are in a suffering condition; and that upon this account, as being yourselves in the body; if the duty respect thy brother, the motive respects thyself; thou art yet in the body; and while you remain in the flesh, you cannot promise yourselves one hour's exemption from troubles; but are exposed to the same common calamities which attend a state of mortality. As it is an argument of comfort to them that are in affliction, that their temptations and trials are common to men (1 Corinthians 10:13); God doth not single them out to encounter with unparalleled affliction. So on the other side it is an incentive to compassion to them that are free, to consider that they are liable to the same temptations; and therefore should measure out the same compassions to their suffering brethren, that they would expect in the same trials; not knowing how soon the cup of trembling may be put into their own hand: to be sure, insensibleness of other men's miseries will hasten it. "They put far away the evil day" (Amos 6:3). They give themselves up to all manner of sensuality, and thereby drown the sense of their brethren's miseries. They are not grieved for the affliction of the Church, it never cost them an hour's sleep, they abated nothing of all their sensual excesses; they never turn aside to shed one tear over bleeding Zion in secret. What follows? "Why," saith God, "therefore now shall they go captive with the first that go captive, and the banquet of them that stretched themselves shall be removed" (v.7); as if God should have said, 'As I live, because you have not pitied your brethren in captivity, you yourselves shall be led away captive, and the next turn shall be yours; and there you shall learn by sense what you would not feel by sympathy.'

And therefore, Christians, set your hearts to the afflictions of the Church and people of God; it is the great duty which the times call for, and I am afraid God is now visiting England and London for the neglect of this duty. We are guilty concerning our brethren in Germany, in Ireland, in England, and Scotland, and in other places. "In that we saw the anguish of their souls, when they besought us, and we would not hear; therefore is this distress come upon us" (Genesis 42:21); we have not grieved their sorrows, nor wept their tears, nor sighed their groans, nor bled their blood; and therefore may fear, lest God should say unto us also, even unto us, with the next that go into captivity, 'They shall go into captivity; with the next that are plundered and spoiled, London shall be plundered and spoiled; with the next that shall be imprisoned, you shall be taken prisoners; with the next that shall be slain with the sword, you shall be slain with the sword; your wives shall be made widows, and your children shall be made fatherless, and your dwellings shall cast you out, and be left desolate'; and therefore let us look to it, and know in this our day the things of our peace, before they be hid from our eyes. Show compassion, that you may not need compassion; or if you need it, you may find it.

In like manner set your hearts to the other lessons which God teaches by his chastisements.

Prize creature comforts more, and surfeit upon them less; be more thankful and less sensual; especially prize a gospel while you have a gospel; prize it by its worth, that you may not prize it by the want; prize it that you may keep it, lest you prize it one day when you cannot recover it. It is a dreadful word, "I will send a famine, not of bread, nor a thirst of water, but of hearing the word of the Lord, and they shall run to and fro, to seek the word of the Lord, and shall not find it" (Amos 8:11-12).

Study self-denial and meekness of spirit. Labour to discover the hidden corruptions of your own hearts. Continue digging into that dunghill and you will find it a bottomless pit; "The heart is deceitful above all things, and desperately wicked, who can know it? I the Lord search the heart" (Jeremiah 17:9-10). Oh entreat the Lord to discover your hearts to you.

Study Scripture evidence for your interest in Christ. Rest not in any evidence which you will not venture your souls upon, if you were to die this moment.

Labour to maintain sweet communion with God; to be able to say with the apostle, and to say truly, "Our communion is with the Father, and with his Son Jesus Christ" (1 John 1:3). Make God your choice, and not your necessity; and labour to maintain such constant converse with him that when you die, you may change your place only, but not your company.

Live up in the exercises of your graces. "Add to your faith virtue, to virtue knowledge, and to knowledge temperance, and to temperance godliness, and to godliness brotherly kindness, and to brotherly kindness charity" (2 Peter 1:5-7). Be adding one grace to another, and one degree of grace to another, and one exercise of grace to another exercise of grace, that God may not add affliction to affliction, and sorrow to sorrow. While others are adding sin to sin, drunkenness to thirst, add grace to grace, "Be steadfast and unmoveable, always abounding in the work of the Lord" (1 Corinthians 15:58).

Acquaint yourselves with God, and good shall come thereby (Job 22:21). Study to know God more and love him better; "Then shall we know, if we follow on to know the Lord" (Hosea 6:3).

Mind, I beseech you, while you are in your strength and peace, the one thing necessary. O take heed of industrious folly, and dishearten not yourselves in the pursuit of trifles! Mind your work.

"Redeem the time, the days are evil" (Ephesians 5:16); O that Christians would study the worth of time! Value a day—say of every hour, yea of every moment, 'This is time.' Redeem time while it may do you good; "Evil days are coming, wherein you will say 'I have no pleasure in them'" (Ecclesiastes 12:1). Yea, the days are evil; evil with sin, evil with sorrow; redeem the time to do good, to receive good, that neither you may be the worse for the times, nor the times for you. Happy shall that man be called who contributes not to the heap of the God-provoking abominations, nor receives impressions from the hypocrisy and prevarication of the present generation.

Study the sufferings of Jesus Christ. Resolve with Paul, "to know nothing but Jesus Christ, and him crucified" (1 Corinthians 2:2). A due contemplation of the cross will heighten Christ's love, and lesson your own sufferings. And labour to get your conversation in heaven, looking for, and hastening to the coming of Christ (2 Peter 3:11-12); say, "Come Lord Jesus, come quickly" (Revelation 22:20).

In a word, brethren, study, and study thoroughly, the sinfulness of sin, emptiness of the creature, and the fullness of Christ.

And in all these and the like lessons, labour for an inward, convincing, experimental, powerful, sweet, abiding teaching.

Content not yourselves, Christians, with a general, slight, superficial, unsavoury, powerless, flitting knowledge. Rest not in notions; be not satisfied with expressions without impressions; nor with impressions that are not abiding impressions, that are like figures written in the sand; this is the ruin of professors. Those professors shall have their names written in the dust, who write divine instructions in the dust.

Know this, if God has a mind to do you good, expect that he should send you into the house of correction, and there teach you with scourges, and write his instructions as it were in blood.

And therefore if you would prevent so severe a discipline, improve your time well in the school of the Word. "While you have the light, walk in the light, lest darkness come upon you" (John 12:35); while you sit under the teachings of the gospel, labour to get knowledge answerable to the means, and grace answerable to your knowledge.

b.) *If you would prevent affliction, labour to be instructed by the chastisements which you see upon other men.* God deals with his children as tutors do with the children of princes, he corrects them upon strangers' backs. Thus God scourged Israel upon the back of the nations round about them; "I have cut off the nations, their towers are desolate, I made their streets waste that none passeth by, their cities are destroyed, so that there is no man, that there is none inhabitant" (Zephaniah 3:6). Their punishment was Israel's caution;

"I said, 'Surely thou wilt fear me, thou wilt receive instruction'" (v.7). The world's judgments are the Church's instructions, and God expected that his people should have made that use of his practical doctrine. God had gracious ends in this dispensation; his severity to strangers was his tender mercy towards Israel; "Behold," as the apostle saith in another case, "the goodness and severity of God" (Romans 11:22); severity to the nations, but goodness towards Israel, had they continued in his goodness and received instruction by their neighbour's destruction. And as God punished Israel upon the nations' backs, so God punished Judah upon Israel's back: "Go ye now to my place in Shiloh, and see what I did to it, for the wickedness of my people Israel" (Jeremiah 7:12). Israel's chastisements should have been Jerusalem's teachings, and by their stripes she should have been healed. For the neglect whereof God is highly displeased, and speaks concerning this in a very angry dialect, "And I saw when, for all the causes whereby backsliding Israel had committed adultery, I had put her away, and given her a bill of divorce; yet her treacherous sister Judah feared not, but went and played the harlot also" (Jeremiah 3:8). God took it ill that Jerusalem should slight the kindness of such a caution, and despise the counsel which was written to her in her sister's blood; as if he had said, 'I would have made Jerusalem wise by Samaria's harms, and taught her by a rod which she only saw; but she feared not; she hardened her heart through unbelief, and either would not understand the caution, or dared me to my face to do my worst, while by her shameless whoredoms she went on to provoke me to jealousy.' This hastened that judgment upon herself which she despised on others; Judah must feel Israel's rod because she would not hear it; as Israel must suffer those judgments on the nations which she herself would not use to her improvement; by those very nations by whom she would not be instructed, she must be destroyed.

So Judah must feel what she feared not at a distance. She that would not tremble at her sister's divorce must suffer divorce herself, and "be judged as women that break wedlock—and bear her own shame for her sins that she had committed more abominable than they" (Ezekiel 16:38,52).

Beloved Christians, if we would prevent the like severity, let us take heed of the like security. God hath been a long time scourging England upon Germany's back, and upon Ireland's back, and upon Scotland's back. God hath for these many years scourged London on the back of all the cities and countries round about us, and God doth daily scourge every one of us in particular upon the back of our suffering brethren, in diverse kinds. His design is that we should fear him, that we should receive instruction. If we altogether fail, we may fear the same rods are preparing for our backs, wherewith they have bled, yea that their rods shall he turned into scorpions to us. We sin worse than others when we sin those very sins for which others have been punished before our faces, and add contempt to their transgressions; and how just will it be with God, if as we aggravate their sins, to aggravate upon us their plagues; that we that would not see and learn, should feel and perish; even particular judgments should be our warnings. Remember Lot's wife; her pillar of salt should season our hearts, that when the judgments of God are abroad in the earth, we that are the inhabitants, not of the earth only—but of Zion also, may learn righteousness.

Even those judgments which the magistrate executes by God's appointment are chiefly for caution to standers by, that others may hear and fear, and do no more any such wickedness; how much more those judgments which the Lord himself doth execute?

2. I come to the second branch of exhortation, which is *to such as yet lie under affliction, and the chastisements of the Almighty.*

Take notice, O thou afflicted soul, what God's design is in afflicting thee, and make it thy design, that thou mayest be taught. "Hear the rod and who hath appointed it" (Micah 6:9). It is the great mistake and folly of men, that they make more haste to get their afflictions removed than sanctified, "The captive exile hasteneth that he may be loosed, that he should not die in the pit" (Isaiah 51:14). Men would fain break prison, or lean out at the window, before God open the door; but this their way is their folly. Men indeed would fain be delivered, but they take not the right course; deliverance belongs unto God: "I am the Lord thy God that divided the sea," and made it a way for my ransomed to pass over, and that when it was most tempestuous, "when the waves thereof roared"; when I will deliver, no obstruction can stand in the way; and yet Israel now in captivity will not look to me: "I am the Lord of Hosts" (v.15), that have all the armies in heaven and earth at my command; and yet when they are besieged with troubles and dangers, I hear not from them; they run to the creature and neglect God; or if they cry to me in their distresses, it is for deliverance only, but not for teaching, though "I have put my words in thy mouth" (v.16); that is, I have given them my laws and statutes, wherein I have made known my design in affliction, that I might humble them, and prove them, and make them know what is in their heart. This is the shortest way to deliverance, and in this path if they had trod, I would have planted the heavens, and laid the foundations of the earth; even the new heavens and the new earth of Jerusalem's restoration, and have said to Zion, 'Thou art my people.'

This is God's method wherein he will own his people, and wherein if they meet him, they shall not stay long for their deliverance. And therefore be wise, O thou afflicted, tossed with tempest, and not comforted; be instructed, lest God's soul depart from thee; make more haste to be taught, than to be delivered, and choose rather to have thy affliction sanctified, than removed. That is observable in Elihu's speech: "Hypocrites in heart heap up wrath"; they add to their own calamities—why? "They cry not when he bindeth them" (Job 36:13).

Consider that *God's design is that he might teach thee by his chastisements*, and if thou crossest God's design, it is just with him to cross thy design. The only way to delay it, is to make too much haste to be delivered, and "he that believeth will not make haste" (Isaiah 28:16).

Consider that *bare deliverance is not the blessing*. I told you before that deliverance is but the common bounty; I tell you more now—deliverance alone may be the fruit of the curse; a man may be delivered in wrath and not in love; deliverance from one affliction may but make way for another, for a greater: affliction may return, like the unclean spirit, with seven more worse than itself; so God threatens an unteachable people; "If by these things ye will not be reformed, but will walk contrary to me," by crossing my design in my chastisements, "then will I walk contrary to you"; I will cross your design, and instead of deliverance, "I will punish you yet seven times more for your sins" (Leviticus 26:23-24). The blessing of correction is instruction; O let not God go till he bless thee (Genesis 32:26).

It is a sad thing to have affliction, but not the *blessing* of affliction: to feel the wood of the cross, but not the good of the cross; to taste the bitter root, but not the sweet fruit of a suffering condition; the curse, but not the cordial. Truly in such a case one affliction may not only make way for another, for more, for greater; but affliction here may make way for damnation hereafter; and as one saith, "By all the fire of affliction in this world, a man may be made fuel for eternal fire." Therefore mind instruction, study the lessons of a suffering condition (as above) and be importunate for nothing so much as to be taught of God, with that special saving teaching which changes the soul into the nature of the truth; and makes the soul holy as that is holy, and pure as that is pure.

3. *To them that have come out of affliction and fiery trials.* Sit down, Christian, and reflect upon thyself, turn in upon thine own heart, and examine thyself. Have teachings accompanied chastisements? Hath the rod budded? Cast up thy accounts; what hast thou learned in the school of affliction? Hath God discovered to thee the sinfulness of sin, the emptiness of the creature, and the fullness of Christ? Is no evil like to the evil of sin? No good like to Jesus Christ? Has the world become an empty vanity, a mockery, a nothing in thine eyes? Can you say, "It is good I have been afflicted" (Psalm 119:71)? Can you point out that good, and say, 'This I had, this I have got by my sufferings; I know divine truth more inwardly, more clearly, it hath a more abiding impression upon my heart'? I would here speak a word to those who through grace do find the fruit of affliction in the savoury and saving teachings of God upon their hearts. Let me, by way of exhortation, commend these duties to you.

a.) *Study to be thankful.* Hath God taught thee as well as chastised thee? O say with David, "What shall I render to the

Lord?" (Psalm 116:12). For consider how great things God hath done to thy soul.

God hath done more for thee than if he had never brought thee into affliction and trouble, or than if he had brought thee out the same day on which he sent thee in. If he had delivered thee upon the first prayer that ever thou madest in thine affliction, it had not been a comparable mercy to his teaching thee by it; prevention and deliverance may be in wrath, but God never teaches the soul, save it be in love.

Again, God hath doubled his mercy and loving-kindness to thee; he hath commanded deliverance and instruction too; a twisted mercy; yea, as deliverance and instruction were the return of prayer, a treble, a multiplied mercy; which should make the heart sing with David, "I will love the Lord, because he hath heard the voice of my supplication" (Psalm 116:1). Double, treble, and multiplied mercy calls for double, treble, and multiplied thankfulness: when God loads us with mercy we should load him with our praises.

Again, instruction is the seal of God, which set upon correction doth seal up adoption and sonship to them that are exercised thereby; the children of affliction are by divine teaching sealed up the children of promise: "If his children forsake my law," speaking of Christ's spiritual seed, "I will visit their transgressions with a rod" (Psalm 89:30,32); that is, I will teach them with the rod; it shall be a rod of instruction to them; that is the children's portion; "If his children forsake me," God deals with you as with sons. Behold, O Christian! God hath done that for thee in thy sufferings which possibly may be denied thee in thy prosperity, given thee an evidence of sonship; he hath made thy suffering time thy sealing time; and hath allured thee and brought thee into the wilderness, and there hath spoken comfortably to thy heart (Job 36:16). Thy Patmos hath been thy paradise, wherein he hath given thee his loves.

God hath consecrated thy sufferings by his teachings: afflictions have taken orders as it were, and stand no longer in the rank of ordinary providences, but serve now in the order of gospel ordinances, officiating in the holy garment of divine promises, and to the same uses. What is the great end and design of the promises? The apostle tells us "that we might be partakers of a divine nature" (2 Peter 1:4), of gracious dispositions and qualities which make the soul resemble God. What the apostle Peter affirms of the promises, the very same doth Paul affirm of God's chastisements, "He for our profit, that we might be partakers of his holiness" (Hebrews 12:10). See by virtue of divine teaching afflictions advanced to the same degree and office with gospel ordinances and promises; so that what hinders, why we may not give those titles of honour to afflictions, which the apostle here gives to the promises, and say, 'There are given unto us exceeding great and precious *afflictions,* that by them we might be partakers of the divine nature,' that is, 'made partakers of his holiness.' See, O thou afflicted soul, by teaching God hath changed the very nature of affliction; he hath turned thy water into wine; a prison, a bed of sickness, into a school, into a temple, wherein he hath taught thee into his own likeness.

And as God hath consecrated thy sufferings, so likewise he hath consecrated thee also by thy sufferings. As it is said of Christ, "He made the captain of our salvation perfect through sufferings" (Hebrews 2:10), he consummated, or perfected him; Christ became a perfect mediator by his cross; hence you hear him cry upon it, "It is finished" (John 19:30). And thus also it may be said of the members of Christ, they are "perfected by sufferings." Chastisement coupled with teaching is the consecration and consummation of the saints, "I fill up," saith St. Paul, "that which is behind of the afflictions of Christ in my flesh" (Colossians 1:24); the after-sufferings of Christ. As Christ as a mediator, so Christ as one body with his members is completed by sufferings. Christ is not full till all his members have had their measure of sufferings. "You have need of patience, that when you have done the will of God, you may inherit the promises" (Hebrews 10:36). When we have done God's will, all is not done; there is somewhat to be suffered, without which the Christian is not in a capacity to receive his inheritance. You have need of patience to carry you through the suffering part of your work, as well as the doing, that so being perfect, you may inherit the promises.

Finally, by adding instruction to correction, God hath crowned thee with the blessing. "Blessed is the man whom thou chastenest and teachest" (Psalm 94:12). God hath turned the crown of thorns into a crown of gold, and set it on thy head, and now brings thee forth wearing this crown, and shows thee, as it were, to the world, as a monument of free grace; proclaiming before thee, "Thus shall it be done to the man whom God delighteth to honour" (cf. Esther 6:6).

Well then, Christian, sit down and consult with thine own soul, what to render for so rich a mercy; and behold, it is resolved to thy hand, "I will deliver thee, and thou shalt glorify me" (Psalm 50:15). God hath not only delivered, but taught thee; now therefore he expects glory from thee.

Glorify God with thy lips, 'I cried to him with my lips, and he was glorified with my tongue.' Let the lip of prayer be turned into the tongue of praise; make your tongues your glory by proclaiming God's glory; be telling what great things God hath done for you; say with David, "Come and hear all ye that fear God, and I will tell you what he hath done for my soul: abundantly utter the memory of his great goodness, make his praise glorious" (Psalm 66:16, 145:7).

Glorify God with thy life, and live his praise. Put all the lessons which thou hast learned into print; "Show forth the praises of him that hath called thee out of darkness into his marvelous light" (1 Peter 2:9); put them in such a legible character, that who so runs may read. Lip-praise is good, but life-praise is better: "He that offereth me praise glorifieth me, and to him that *ordereth his conversation aright* will I shew the salvation of God" (Psalm 50:23). It is good to speak so that standers-by may be God's witnesses and yours, that you are taught of God; and say, "Lo what hath God wrought?" (Numbers 23:23). How holily, and humbly, and fruitfully, and self-denyingly do these servants of God walk since they came out of tribulation? Live so that you may take off the scandal of the cross of Christ, and bring men into love with a suffering condition. "Let your light shine before men, that they may see your good works, and glorify your Father which is in heaven" (Matthew 5:16).

Again, now God hath taught thee, be ready to teach others. It is a debt which you owe to all you converse with,

"When thou art converted, strengthen thy brethren" (Luke 22:32). Communicate what God hath taught thee to thy yoke-fellow, children, and others, upon all seasonable opportunities. Sanctified knowledge is communicative; "freely thou hast received, freely give" (Matthew 10:8). God never lighted this candle that it should be put under the bed of pleasure, or the bushel of profit; but that it may be put into the candlestick of thy conversation, and so "shine before men, that they may see and glorify thy Father which is in heaven" (Matthew 5:16). This is indeed to glorify God.

b.) *Labour to preserve the teachings of God upon thy spirit.* Study how to maintain that sweet gracious frame of heart into which God hath taught thee by affliction. It is the duty which Christians should practise as often as they come from the Word, or any other divine ordinance. When we come out of a sabbath, we should sit down and observe with what frame of spirit God sends us away from the ordinance. If the ordinance hath left no savoury gracious impression upon the heart, to lie in the dust, and mourn, and commune with our own hearts, and lament after God. If there be an ordinance frame, we should rejoice in it, bless God for it, and labour to keep up such a frame upon the heart till the next solemn approach to God. And how much more should it be our care, when we come out of God's furnace, to labour to maintain that melting frame of heart, that life and vigour which we have brought with us out of affliction. "Look to yourselves, that ye lose not those things which God hath wrought in you" (2 John 1:8). To that end take these helps:

[1.] *Be often reading over the lessons which God hath taught you;* frequently revive the remembrance of them in your heads and work the impressions of them upon your hearts. You have need to take much pains with yourselves, to keep the teachings of God alive upon your spirits, "The heart is deceitful above all things, and desperately wicked" (Jeremiah 17:9). There is much of a Pharaoh-like disposition in every man, very prone to harden when the storm is over. It is sad and wonderful to consider how a corruption will lie as if it were quite dead while danger and death are before us, and how suddenly and powerfully it will revive and betray the soul when the danger is over. That caution which God by

Moses gave the Israelites in the wilderness, may make every wise Christian tremble, "I know their imaginations, which they go about even now, before I have brought them into the land, which I sware" (Deuteronomy 31:21). Their hearts were secretly scheming their lusts, even while they were yet smarting under the rod; and in the howling wilderness they are forecasting how to satisfy sense and serve their carnal interests, when they should come into the land that flowed with milk and honey. Possibly, these were not down-right resolves; but saith the Lord, "I know their imaginations." O my brethren, we should hearken to the whisperings of lust in our own bosoms, and labour to suppress them; for if there are now such floatings of sin in the imagination, what will there be when enlargement shall present temptations and opportunities? And therefore "keep we our hearts with all diligence, for out of them come the issues of life" (Proverbs 4:23).

[2.] *Renew often the remembrance of the sharpness and bitterness of the affliction;* it will be a good corrective to sensuality, and give check to sinful excesses. The flesh will quickly grow wanton when it finds ease; Jeshurun, when the neck was got from under the yoke, quickly "waxed fat and kicked" (Deuteronomy 32:15): they soon forgot his works. They quickly forgot a barren wilderness, in a land that flowed with milk and honey. They waited not for his counsel; they grew weary of it when once free from correction, and chose rather to walk by the dictate of their own lusts, than of God's laws, till at length God grew as weary (if I may so say) of counseling, as they were of being counseled; and "gave them up to their own hearts' lusts, to walk in their own counsels" (Psalm 81:12). They that would not live by God's counsels should perish by their own. And therefore, you that are come out of the house of bondage, remember the sorrows of a suffering condition; set not your heart so much upon the pleasure of your present enlargement, as upon the bitterness of your former captivity. The Church found great advantage in it, when returned from Babylon, "Remembering mine affliction and my misery, the wormwood and the gall; my soul hath them *continually* in remembrance" (Lamentations 3:19-20). And what was the fruit of it? It follows, "and is humbled in me" (v.20b). And that is not all, as remembrance of affliction preserved humility, so humility strengthened faith: "This I recall to mind, therefore have I *hope*; tribulation wrought patience, and patience experience, and experience *hope*," and so forth (Lamentations 3:21).

[3.] *Call often to mind the sad discourses and reasonings, the fears and tremblings, which you have had in your bosoms in the times of trouble and distress.* Thus the Church, "I forgat prosperity" (Lamentations 3:17); she had been so long in a suffering condition, that now she can scarce remember that ever she saw a good day in all her life; and at length she sits down, and giveth herself up to despair, "And I said, my strength and my hope is perished from the Lord" (v.18). She remembered what unbelieving conclusions she made in her affliction; and so the prophet Jeremiah, "Waters flowed over mine head; then I said, 'I am cut off'" (Lamentations 3:54); when he began to sink in the mire, he remembered how his heart began to sink with fear; he called to mind what faithless language his heart spoke, "I said, 'I am cut off.'"

Hezekiah makes a large narrative of what discourses he had in his own soul when he had received the sentence of death, and left it in writing to all posterity: "The writing of Hezekiah, king of Judah, when he had been sick, I said in the cutting off of my days," what did he say? "I shall go to the gates of the grave; I am deprived of the residue of my years; mine age is departed" (Isaiah 38:9-10), and a great deal more to that purpose; the sum whereof is this, 'I shall die, I shall die. I must take my leave of this world, and worms must eat my flesh in the grave,' and so forth. Such uncomely words he uttered; but he remembered them afterward, and is contented to shame himself for them to all the world. He puts his complaints in print, that he may humble himself, and caution, yea and comfort, others.

Thus, Christians, should we do, we should call to mind our *saids*; we should sit down and recount the impatience, murmurs, and unbelief; the love of a present world, the fear of death, the hard thoughts of God; all the irregularities and distempers of our own spirits in the time of tribulation. Doubtless it would be of singular use, as to humble our souls and check corruption, so to endear and preserve the teachings of God upon your souls. While you might tune David's thanksgiving (conceived upon some such like occasion), "Good and upright is the Lord, therefore will he *teach sinners* in the way" (Psalm 25:8); as much as to say, 'I sinned against the Lord in my affliction by my impatience, unbelief, unhumbledness, and so forth, yet he was pleased, not altogether to leave me without the teachings of his Spirit—not because I was good, but because he was good; not because I pleased him, but because mercy pleased him; not because I was upright before him, but because he was upright. True and faithful to his own promise, hath he done it, good and upright is the Lord, and therefore *he* hath *taught* me in the way.'

[4.] *Remember your vows.* When God by affliction showed you your folly, discovered to you the hidden corruption of your hearts, and brought your ways and doings to remembrance, which were not good, you were ashamed, yea, even confounded; and said, as it is in Job, "Lord, wherein I have done wickedly, I will do so no more" (Job 34:32). But take heed it be not with you as it was with backsliding Israel, of whom God thus complained: "Of old time I have broken thy yoke, and burst thy bands, and thou saidst, 'I will not transgress'" (Jeremiah 2:20).

I brought thee (as if he had said) hundreds of years since, out of the land of Egypt, out of the house of bondage, and then thou made me fair promises. "I remember the kindness of thy youth, the love of thine espousals" (Jeremiah 2:2); thou saidst, "I will do so no more" (Job 34:32); Lord, I will be covetous no more, idolatrous no more, adulterous no more. I will murmur no more; I will no more depart from thee, "Thou art the guide of my youth" (Jeremiah 3:4). Good words, had she been as good as her word: but O read what follows, and tremble! "When upon every high hill, and under every green tree, thou wanderest, playing the harlot" (Jeremiah 2:20). No sooner had her old heart and her old temptations met, but presently they fell into mutual embraces; and this is the temper of our hearts, we are very good while we are in affliction, and promise fair; but no sooner is the trial over, but we forget God's teachings and our own vows, and return into the same course and fashion of conversation as before. Now therefore, if you would preserve the teachings of God upon your spirits, sit down, remember your vows; and spreading them before the Lord, say with David, "I will pay thee my vows, which my lips have uttered, and my mouth hath spoken, when I was in trouble" (Psalm 66:13-14).

[5.] If you would preserve the teachings of God upon your heart, *attend constantly and conscientiously upon the ministry of the Word.* The truth is, the Word and the rod teach the same lessons. The rod many times is but the Word's *remembrancer;* and therefore as the rod quickens the Word, so the Word will revive and sanctify the teachings of the rod; they mutually help to set on one another with deeper impressions. And therefore "Hear wisdom, watching daily at her gates, waiting at the posts of her doors" (Proverbs 8:33-34), if thou wilt be blessed. It will be of a twofold advantage—

First. It will help your memories. As the rod repeats the Word, so the Word will repeat the instructions of the rod; the gospel will bring to remembrance what you have learned in the school of affliction.

Second. It will quicken affection. To hear that repeated by the still small voice of the gospel, which before God taught you in the voice of thunder; this cannot but affect, and make you bespeak the gospel, as once the Israelites did Moses, "Speak thou unto us all that the Lord our God shall speak unto thee, and we wilt hear it and do it, but let us not hear the voice of God any more," that terrible voice of judgment, "lest we die" (Deuteronomy 5:27; Exodus 20:18-19). And certainly God will take it as well at your hands as he did at Israel's, and will answer in some such language; "I have heard the voice of this people, they have well said all that they have spoken: O that there were such an heart in them, that they would fear me, and keep my commandments, that it might be well with them" (Deuteronomy 5:28-29), and that I might not bring upon them such evils as I have done, anymore!

[6.] *Be often feeding that frame of heart which God hath taught thee into;* do by it as thou daily beggest God would do by thee; give it day by day its daily bread (Matthew 6:11).

Maintain meditations suitable to the nature of that grace which thou wouldst maintain; threatenings, promises, truths, and Scripture considerations agreeable to the lesson. Take heed of feeding corruption with thoughts of the sweetness that is in sin; take heed also of starving grace by withdrawing from it suitable nourishment. You will require the blood of your infants that are starved at the nurses' hands; will not God be much more jealous over the births and issues of his own Spirit? Meditate much upon the sinfulness of sin, the emptiness of the creature, the fullness of Christ, the exquisiteness of his sufferings, the severity of the last judgment, the torments of hell, the joys of heaven, the infinite perfections of the divine nature, and the horror of eternity. Rich in meditation and rich in grace.

[7.] *And lastly, be much in prayer.* As it was not enough for God to make the first creation, but he must "uphold it by the word of his power" (Hebrews 1:3), or else it would quickly have returned into its first nothing; so it is with the second creation, Christ is the finisher as well as the author of grace (Hebrews 12:2); he that hath begun a good work in you, must perfect it (Philippians 1:6). Stability only comes from the unchangeable God; therefore pray that God would put his unchangeableness upon you. Pray as Luther was in the habit of praying, "Confirm, O Lord, in us what thou hast wrought, and perfect the work thou hast begun in us to thy glory, Amen." He seems to have taken this out of Psalm 68:28, "Strengthen, O God, that which thou hast wrought in us." Pray that prayer which David prayed over that liberal frame of heart which God had formed in his people, for the service of the temple: "O Lord God of Abraham, and Isaac, and Jacob, our fathers, keep this forever in the imagination of the thoughts of the heart of thy people, and prepare (or *establish*) their heart unto thee" (1 Chronicles 29:18). Oh be earnest with God for stability of heart, that thy goodness may not be as a morning cloud, and as the early dew; but that it may, in some proportion, resemble the author of it, and be the same yesterday, and today, and forever (Hebrews 13:8).

In summary, by all these means and helps, and what other God hath sanctified for this gracious end, labor, Christians, to be such out of your afflictions, as you promised God and yourselves to be when you were in them, so that the fruit of chastening may be repentance never to be repented of. Having in your troubles repented of your sins, take heed when you are delivered, that you repent not of your repentance.

c.) I come now to the third duty of them that are come of out afflictions: *pray for the afflicted*. And when you pray, say, 'Lord teach them, as well as correct them, that they may be blessed.' O pray thus for England; she hath been a long time sorely chastised of the Lord, and yet hath been all this while "like a bullock unaccustomed to the yoke" (Jeremiah 31:18). O pray, "Turn us, Lord, and we shall be turned, thou art the Lord our God" (Lamentations 5:21). Pray that God would teach England in this day of her visitation the things of her peace, before they be hid from her eyes. O pray that we may be *instructed*, lest God depart from us. If correction is not accompanied with instruction; if England is not at length reformed by all the judgments of God upon her, then she has already seen her best days, and may expect to be "made desolate, a land not inhabited" (Jeremiah 6:8); there is no balm for our pain, neither any physician that can heal our malady.

Pray thus for all your friends who are or have been in the furnace of affliction; pray that they may come forth as gold purified seven times in the fire, that they may lose nothing there but their rust and dross. One great use which Christians should make of reading the Scriptures is to learn the language of prayer. O that the professors of this age would in this particular, learn *what* to pray, and *how* to pray for their brethren in tribulation. O that they would censure less, and pray more; and instead of speaking one *of* another, speak more one *to* another, and one *for* another. That was the good old way, "Then they that feared the Lord spake often one to another" (Malachi 3:16). But now the tender, praying, healing, restoring Spirit is departed; and if Christians stir not up themselves to call it back again, it is a sad presage that God is departing too; and woe unto us when God departs from us. We judge before we enquire, and reject before we admonish, our brethren upon vain surmises are to us as heathens and publicans, before we have been to them

as Christians and fellow members. And this we think becomes us, and we take a kind of pride and contentment in it.
But O to inform, to convince, to exhort, to pray, to put the
bone that is out in joint again, this is to act like the disciples
of Christ; to show ourselves Christians indeed, professors not
of the letter, but of the Spirit, and would gain our brethren
instead of blasting them.

Finally, I would also address such as cannot evidence to
their own souls that chastening hath been accompanied with
divine teaching in any gospel proportion, or at least are not
deeply sensible of the lack of it. Here is a word of exhortation for them, suffer it I beseech you. Roll yourselves in the
dust before the Lord; smite upon your thigh; sigh with the
breaking of your loins, and cry out with Ephraim, "Thou
hast chastised me and I was chastised, as a bullock unaccustomed to the yoke" (Jeremiah 31:18); I have felt the blows of
God, but that is all; I have received no more instruction by
all my correction than a brute beast; or if I had, I have quickly lost it; it is fled like a bird, from the birth, and from the
womb, and from the conception; it is like the untimely fruit
of a woman that never saw the sun.

Truly thou hast cause to sit down, and even wish for thy
affliction again. God had put himself into thy hands as it
were, and thou hast let him go without the blessing, the
blessing of saving instruction. How mayest thou even wish,
'O that I were in prison again, in my sick bed again, in banishment again.' However, humble thyself greatly before the
Lord, and wrestle mightily for the *after teachings* of God upon thy heart. Pray, "Turn me Lord, and I shall be turned, for
thou art the Lord my God" (Lamentations 5:21); what affliction hath not done, Lord do thou— "turn me, and I shall be
turned"; that so thy soul may yet speak to the praise of free
grace: "After that I returned I repented, and *after* that I was
instructed, I smote upon my thigh; I was ashamed, yea even
confounded, because I did bear the reproach of my youth"
(Jeremiah 31:19). Urge the Lord, as Sampson did after his
victory, "Thou hast given this great deliverance into the hand
of thy servant, and shall I now die for thirst, and fall into the
hand of the uncircumcised?" (Judges 15:18). Say unto him,
'Lord, thou hast given thy servant this great deliverance from

danger and death, and shall I now perish for want of teaching, and go down to hell among the uncircumcised?' "Teach me thy way, O Lord, I will walk in thy truth; unite my heart to fear thy name" (Psalm 86:11). In a word, desire the Lord that he would do all the work, and then take all the glory; say, 'Lord teach me as well as deliver me, and I shall be blessed.'

4. The fourth and last branch of exhortation is to parents and governors—to exhort them in the education of their children to imitate God, and that in two things:

a.) *Afford your children due correction.* It is the counsel of the Holy Ghost, "Chasten thy son while there is hope, and let not thy soul spare for his crying" (Proverbs 19:18). Behold, God counsels you that are parents to do with your children as he doth with his; wisely to use the discipline of the rod, before vicious dispositions grow into habits, and folly be so deeply rooted that the rod of correction will not drive it out. "Error and folly," saith one very well, "are the knots of Satan with which he ties sinners to the stake to be burnt in hell"; and these knots are easiest cut betimes; or if you should make the child bleed in cutting of them, let it not cause you to withdraw your hand; for so it follows, "Chasten thy son, and let not thy soul spare for his crying": it is not only foolish, but cruel pity to forbear correction for a few childish tears; to suffer the child to wail in hell for sin, rather than to shed a few tears for the preventing of it. Foolish fathers and mothers call this love, but the Father of Spirits calls it hatred: "He that spareth the rod, hateth his son" (Proverbs 13:24). Surely there is nothing so ill-spared as that whereby the child is bettered, such sparing is hatred; and because you hate your children in not correcting them, they may come afterwards to hate you for not correcting them.

But this is not all; the parent's leniency in this case makes way for God's severity: pity to the flesh is cruelty to the soul; so the Hebrew may be rendered, "Spare not to his destruction, or to cause him to die"; that is, to occasion his destruction. The foolish indulgence of the parent may be, and often is, the death of the child—eternal death. Parents spare their children in their folly to the destruction both of body and soul.

And this may help us to expound that other parallel text, "Withhold not correction from the child, for if thou beat him with the rod he shall not die" (Proverbs 23:13). The meaning may be either that correction will not kill him; the rod will break no bones; so preventing and reproving at once the silly and sinful tenderness of fond parents, who think if they should correct their children, they would presently die of it; they are as afraid to use the rod as if it were a sword. Nay, but saith the Holy Ghost, fear not correction, for behold, the strokes of the rod are not the strokes of death: it is but a rod, it is not a serpent, take it into thy hand; it may smart, it will not sting. To obviate the fear of parents in this case, God himself giveth his word for it, "He shall not die."

This may be the meaning, or else (which I rather conceive) the words may be a motive drawn from the fruit of correction; "Withhold not correction from the child"; why? "He shall not die," in other words it may be, and (through divine blessing accompanying it) is often a means to *prevent* death; it may prevent the first and second death, to which the child is exposed by the sinful indulgence of the parent. The word used in this place, saith one, seems to note an immortality; so that "He shall not die," is all one as if the Holy Ghost had said, 'He shall live forever,' the rod on the flesh shall be a means to save the soul in the day of the Lord Jesus. "We an chastened that we should not be condemned with the world" (1 Corinthians 11:32). "Such smitings," as David saith in another case, "shall be a kindness" (Psalm 141:5); and such rebukes are so far from breaking the head, that they shall be an excellent oil which shall cure, and give life. Even the philosopher could say, "Correction is a kind of physic or medicine."

Alas, our children are sick, and cruel is that mercy which will suffer them to die, yea eternally, rather than disgust their palates with a little bitter physic! They are apes and monkeys in the form of men and women, who thus hug their little ones to death; parricides rather than parents; of whom we may say, as sometime the Roman emperor said of Herod, when he heard that he had murdered his own son among the rest of the infants in Bethlehem, that so he might be sure to destroy the King of the Jews, "Surely it is better to be such people's swine than their sons."

O hateful indulgence an merciless pity, to lose a child for lack of correction! Such parents throw both the rod and the child into the fire at once; the rod into the fire of the chimney, and the child into the fire of hell. This is not done like God, for "whom the Lord loveth he chasteneth, and scourgeth every son whom he receiveth" (Hebrews 12:6); and so doth every wise loving parent; "He that spareth the rod hateth his son, but he that loveth him chasteneth him betimes" (Proverbs 13:24). As moths are beaten out of a garment with a rod, so must vices out of children's hearts. And for lack of this disciplinary love, how have some children accused their parents on their death-bed, yea at the gallows! And how many do and will curse them in hell, in some such language as Cyprian supposes infants to complain of their parents who denied them baptism: "The treacherous fondness of our parents hath brought us into these torments; our fathers and mothers have been our murderers; they that gave us our natural life have deprived us of a better; and they that would not correct us with the rod, have occasioned us now to be tormented with scorpions."

Yea, even in this life, how do many godly parents smart for their fondness, because they will not make their children smart for their folly. Eli and David would not so much as rebuke their sons; and God gave them rebukes in their sons. It is said of Eli, "His sons made themselves vile, and he *restrained* them not" (1 Samuel 3:13); the Hebrew has it, "He *frowned* not upon them." Oh sad—for want of a frown, to destroy a soul!

I am much afraid, this unchristian, yea unnatural indulgence of parents, is the fountain of all that confusion under which England at this time reels and staggers like a drunken man. And for this very sin (at least for this among others, yea, and for this above others) God is visiting all the families of the land, from the throne to the poorest cottage. Parents have laid the foundation of their own sorrows, their children's ruin, and the desolation of the nation, in the looseness and delicacy of their education, and yet are not sensible of it to this day. Therefore God doth cross us in our righteous desires; we have walked, even in this point, exceedingly contrary to God and to his discipline; and therefore God is walking contrary to us, and is punishing us seven times more for this iniquity. And therefore O that parents would at length awaken themselves, to follow both the pattern and precept of their heavenly Father, who, as "he correcteth whom he loveth," so he commands them to correct if they love their children. "Withhold not correction from the child; for if thou correct him with the rod he shall not die" (Proverbs 23:13). And it is further worth observation, that the same word in the original, which is translated "withhold", signifies also "to forbid"; meeting with another distemper in parents, who as they will not correct their children themselves, so also they forbid others to correct them, under whose tuition they put them, as if they were afraid their children would not have sin enough here, nor hell enough hereafter, they lay in caveats against the means which God hath sanctified for their reclaiming. Parents, take heed that when you commit your children to others' hands, you do not in the meanwhile hold their hands; if thou judgest them not wise, why dost thou choose them? If thou choose them, why dost thou not trust them? Well then, if the rod be in thine own hand, withhold it not; if in thy friend's hand, forbid it not. Certainly there is great need of this duty, which the Spirit of God doth frequently inculcate all through the Proverbs.

b.) And secondly, if you would have your children happy, *add instruction to correction*. Imitate God in this part of paternal discipline also; let chastisement and instruction go together—it is what the Holy Ghost urges upon you, "Bring them up in the nurture and admonition of the Lord" (Ephesians 6:4).

There are two words relating to both these parental duties; in the "nurture" or *correction*; and it is added, "of the Lord": that is, either in the chastisement with which the Lord exercises his children; or in the chastisement which the Lord commands earthly parents to exercise towards their children; this is the first duty, of which we have already addressed. And then there is another word, which holds forth the end and design of parental correction; that is the "admonition" or *instruction* of the Lord; counsels and instructions taken out of the Word of God, or such as are approved of by God. The sum is this, that while we chasten the flesh, we should labour to inform and form the mind and spirit, by infusing right principles, pressing and urging upon their tender hearts counsel, reproof, and instruction as the matter requires.

This is the duty of parents, to imitate God, to let instruction expound correction; and with a rod in the hand, and a word in the mouth, to train up their children to life eternal. A dumb rod is but a brutish discipline, and will certainly leave them more brutish than it found them. Chastisement without teaching, may sooner break the bones than the heart; it may mortify the flesh, but not corruption; extinguish nature, but never beget grace. But the rod *and* reproof give wisdom. As instruction added to correction makes excellent Christians, so also does it make good children.

There are parents that are severe and crusty enough to their children; they spare for no blows. Instead of breaking them of their wills by a wise and moderate correction, they are ready to break their bones, and their necks too sometimes, in their passions; but they never mind the other branch of paternal discipline, *instruction and admonition*. Of such parents I suppose the apostle speaks, "We have had fathers of our flesh, who corrected and chastened us after their own pleasure" (Hebrews 12:9-10). He is not speaking of all parents, but his meaning is, there are such men and women in the world who are most unlike to God, and in smiting their children rather please themselves than profit their children; he for our profit, but they after their own pleasure, to give vent to their passion, and satisfy their vindictive rage and fury. And when is that? Truly when the rod and reproof do not go together, it is an argument that there is more passion than judgment, more lust than love, in such chastisements. Such parents do rather betray their own folly, than take a course to make their children wise. The rod and reproof give wisdom; neither alone will do it. The rod without reproof will harden the heart and teach children sooner to hate their parents than to hate sin, while reproof without the rod will oftentimes leave no impression. It is divine truth alone that must be the instrument which works saving grace in the heart, "Sanctify them with thy truth, thy word is truth"

(John 17:17). It is the commendation of Timothy's mother, that from his very infancy, she instructed him in the Scriptures, "which were able to make him wise to salvation" (2 Timothy 3:15). When there is a divine sentence in the mouth of the rod, it brings wisdom and life with it.

And therefore, O that parents would imitate the Father of Spirits in this blessed art of paternal discipline, join the word of instruction to the rod of correction; teach as well as chastise, "Reprove, rebuke, exhort with all long-suffering and doctrine" (2 Timothy 4:2). O that every child might have cause to give their parents that commendation which once Augustine gave his mother, in reference to his baptism, "My mother labored with my everlasting salvation with more tenderness and sorrow, than ever she did with my first birth." O that natural parents could bespeak the fruit of their loins, as St. Paul bespeaks his Galatians, "My little children, of whom I travail in birth again until Christ be formed in you" (Galatians 4:19); so that they might rejoice in the second more than they ever did in the first birth. Beloved, this is done by *the Word and the rod.* "Correct thy son and he shall give thee rest, yea he shall give delight unto thy soul" (Proverbs 29:17). What greater delight than to see your children walking in truth, and to think thus with yourselves, that so many children God hath given you, so many children you have brought up for God, and so many heirs for the kingdom of heaven! Well, chastise and teach them out of the law of God, and thy children shall be blessed. Which, that they may, indeed take one short caution more, and that is—

Add prayer to instruction. As teaching should accompany chastisement, so prayer should accompany teaching. God need use only the rod and the Word because the blessing is in his own hand; he can command a blessing. It is not so with us, as Paul may plant, and Apollos may water, but God must give the increase (1 Corinthians 3:6); so the father may correct, the mother may instruct, both may do both, but God must give the blessing. So therefore Christian parents, while they add instruction to correction, should add prayer to instruction; means are ours, success is God's; and therefore let us put the rod into the hand of instruction, instruction into the hand of prayer, and all into the hand of God. I knew a worthy gracious lady who would never use the rod; but, as with much pious instruction before; so after would cause the child (if of capacity) or ever it stirred solemnly to kneel down, and beg a blessing of God upon it. Go you and do likewise; pray and teach your children to pray, that God would so bless correction and instruction, that both may make you and your children blessed. Amen.

SCRIPTURE INDEX

GLOSSARY

abate – to lessen or weaken in intensity; to diminish

amiable – agreeable, friendly, or likeable

acquit – to release from an obligation; to settle or satisfy

apostasy – abandonment of one's former religious beliefs

bandy – to bounce around

beatific – blessed, blissful

bespeak – to foretell; to indicate or address

betimes – within a short time; soon

bridewell – prison

brimstone – sulfur

casuistical – applying general ethical principles to specific situations

caveat – a warning or admonition; a caution

censure – a strong reprimand or expression of disapproval

churl – a rude, base, boorish person

comely – proper, suitable, becoming

congruous – appropriate or fitting; harmonious

consecrate – to set apart or declare sacred or for sacred use

conventicle – a secret (usually unlawful) religious assembly

cordial – (adj.) heartfelt or sincere

creature – (adj.) anything than ministers to man's comforts

cross – (v.) to oppose, thwart, vex, or frustrate

despondent – discouraged, melancholy, disheartened

diffidence – distrustful

dispensation – something given to man by God

dubious – doubtful or questioning

dross – impurities removed from metal when it is smelted

enmity – a state of hostility between two parties

ere – before

exhort – to encourage, recommend, or advise

exigence – a need inherent to a situation

experimental – something based on one's own experience

fain – willingly, happily, eagerly

flesh-pot – a place offering sensual pleasures or entertainment

flitting – moving swiftly from place to place

forwardness – stubbornly contrary or oppositional

gage – a token which signals a readiness to fight

gall – bile; something bitter or severe

gallows – a platform constructed for execution by hanging

gird – to bind (as with a belt); to prepare oneself for action

gout – a painful inflammation of the joints

governor – a person charged with the upbringing of children

heathen – a person who is not religious

husbandry – farming; the management of a household

impenitent – not feeling a sense of remorse for one's sins

importunity – marked by repeated insistent requests

impotence – utter inability to do something

indictment – a charge or accusation

infamy – well-known for a shameful or outrageous act

ingenuity – frankness, sincerity; without cunning or guile

iniquity – sin, wickedness

inure – to habituate to something undesirable by prolonged exposure

Magna Carta – a document that outlines a people's basic rights

malefactor – an evildoer or criminal

munition – war materiel such as weapons or fortification

nigh – near

nonplussed – bewildered, perplexed, or at a loss

noxious – harmful, toxic, or corrupting

obduration – hardness

obviate – to render unnecessary

ordinance – prescribed public practices of the church; for example baptism or sharing in the Communion meal

parley – (n.) a discussion of terms with an enemy

parricide – a person who murders a close relative

penitent – (adj.) remorseful

peradventure – uncertainty or doubt

peremptory – putting an end to debate; irrefutable

physic – a medicine or drug

pious – commendable, worthy, or devout

precept – a rule or principle for action

prevaricate – to lie

prodigal – wasteful; lavishly abundant

professor – a person who claims to be a Christian

propound – to set forth for consideration

publican – a tax collector; a tavern-keeper

quarto – a book which is one quarter the size of a sheet of paper

quietus est – release from a debt or obligation

rankle – to inflame, fester, or irritate

regenerate – (adj.) reborn spiritually

reins – kidneys (formerly considered the seat of affections)

reproach – (n.) blame, disgrace, or shame; rebuke

reprobate – (adj.) rejected by God; destined for damnation

savoury – pleasant; respectable

sensual – pertaining to the gratifying of the senses

Septuagint – a Greek translation of the Hebrew Scriptures

signal – (adj.) conspicuously distinguished

straits – difficult or adverse circumstances

stranguary – a slow and painful discharge of urine

subservient – subordinate; useful in promoting an end

sublunary – "beneath the moon"; earthly

supercilious – feeling or showing proud haughtiness

supersedeas – an order to cease from work

supplication – a humble and earnest prayer for something

surfeit – to eat or drink to excess; to engorge

surmise – to infer something without seeing all the evidence

Tophet – an extremely unpleasant place or condition; Hell

tuition – guardianship; instruction or teaching

tractable – easily managed or governed; malleable

travail – (n.) difficult work; tribulation; anguish; childbirth

unsavoury – objectionable, distasteful; disagreeable

vex – to trouble, perplex, or annoy; to bring suffering to

vicissitude – a change in circumstances that often connotes misfortune

want – lack, be in need of something

wanton – immoral or lewd; unrestrained; rebellious; cruel

wax – (v.) to increase gradually in size, number, or intensity

wont – accustomed to; in the habit of doing something

wormwood – something harsh or bitter; a painful experience

wile – a trick intended to deceive or ensnare

THE DANGER OF PROSPERITY

William Bates

In *The Danger of Prosperity*, William Bates insightfully teaches Christians how wealth, honour, and fame often contribute to the downfall of the unwary. He challenges his readers—with the tender encouragement of a shepherd—to carefully consider the ways in which the abuse of prosperity is both deadly and destructive. He provides numerous helps that Christians who enjoy God's hand of blessing can use to avoid its sinful abuse and improve it to God's glory and their eternal advantage.
ISBN: 978-1463506643. 116 pp. Paperback. $8.99

DAILY COMMUNION WITH GOD

Matthew Henry

In *Daily Communion with God*, Matthew Henry shows how to begin each day with God in quiet prayer and meditation upon Scripture. He then shows how to take that same spirit into the day's events while still reflecting upon his duty to honour God in thought, word, and deed. Finally, the author shows how believers are to close the day with God by prayerful consideration of the day's successes and failures, with an eye toward our continual dependence upon him for strength and mercy.
ISBN: 978-1463666088. 154 pp. Paperback. $8.99

THE CASE AND CURE OF A DESERTED SOUL

Joseph Symonds

In *The Case and Cure of a Deserted Soul*, Joseph Symonds explores the nature, causes, and treatment of spiritual depression—a state that arises when God seems to hide his face, leaving the Christian to walk alone in a "dark night of the soul." Every aspect of this condition is examined with a surgeon's precision, a philosopher's insight, and the Word of God's wisdom on how to gain a firmer footing and emerge from this melancholy hour with renewed strength and vivacity.
ISBN: 978-1467917629. 306 pp. Paperback. $14.99

Printed in Dunstable, United Kingdom

69048843R00085